MW01233397

Front Row Seats to Crazy

Front Row Seats to Crazy

Helena L. Rouhe

Copyright © 2016 Helena L. Rouhe
All rights reserved.

ISBN-13: 9781523205356
ISBN-10: 1523205350

Front Row Seats to Crazy

Helena Rouhe

"Everybody does have a book in them, but in
most cases that's where it should stay."

—Christopher Hitchens

I LOVE TO TELL STORIES. I have entertained many people with embarrassing stories of myself (I have many), my family, circumstances I have witnessed… you get the idea. The stories I like to tell are intended to entertain and encourage conversation.

Several years ago my life turned upside down, and the people close to me suggested I share my story with others because they thought it was inspiring. Telling my story is one thing, writing it is another, and publishing is terrifying. It is why I think Mr. Hitchens had a point: writing a compelling story is difficult and most don't succeed.

My parents died eighteen days apart. They lived for the moment and didn't like to plan for the future. When the music stopped, I was left with all the luggage and no place to sit down. This book is my impressions of my life and how my parents influenced me both in life and in death. Although I witnessed many amazing things, I feel the label *crazy* is more a reflection of how I felt about the events I describe rather than a state of mind.

As a marriage and family therapist, I help people with their relationship issues. Relationships affect us all. If you have unfinished business from the past, current relationships will be affected: an effect that can wreak havoc on a person's life. I consider it a great honor to work with people who have determined that they want to resolve the issues that plague them. I consider myself an educated companion who is given an opportunity to walk with someone as we sort out their personal struggles.

I am truly inspired by the people who wrestle with difficult circumstances. They work to take responsibility for their feelings, their reactions, and their thought processes, and have a willingness to change the way they respond to negative circumstances, thereby becoming healthier individuals. While working as a therapist, I have been inspired to get through tough personal times because my clients, who had much tougher circumstances, were willing to do the same.

My specialty is working with women who struggle with addiction. I've spent most of my career working in a residential treatment center environment for women struggling with any combination of drug and/or alcohol addiction, trauma, and/or eating disorders. These women are amazing and truly inspirational. But my understanding of how to work with people struggling mentally reached a new level of awareness when I worked in a voluntary psychiatric hospital. Prior to this experience I had both a book knowledge of mental disorders and a personal knowledge, but I lacked a working knowledge. I had the opportunity to work with people who had accomplished careers in this field, and their insights on day-to-day treatment were incredible. I feel it's important for me to share the key points of what I learned because it is directly relevant to what inspired me to write this book.

I have two masters of arts degrees in psychology. The first is in visual cognitive psychology and the second I have already discussed, MFT (counseling). Cognitive psychology is the study of how people perceive their environment. My focus on visual cognition allowed me to work in a lab studying how vision and depth perception changes with age and how the physical changes manifest themselves in day-to-day actions, confidence levels, and behaviors. This was incredibly interesting to me because it allowed me to study neuroscience in both what is known about neural functioning and what current science speculates might be happening.

Mind versus neural anatomy has always been a topic of interest for me because my father was a neurosurgeon. I spent my childhood hearing his patients' stories of overcoming terrible disease or traumatic accidents. Their recovery, in part, was due to my father being a talented surgeon who cared deeply about his patients. He never gave up or turned away a tough case. Our dinner discussions often revolved around his day and the challenges he faced. What always stood out to me was the empathy he had for his patients' circumstances. He truly wanted everyone to get better, and it was hard on him when someone did not recover.

Inspired by the neurosurgeon in my life, I found myself in a lab studying brain function. However, the lab was situated in a dark room in a basement of the psychology building, and my need to be outside in the sun eventually overtook my curiosity. So instead of staying to complete my PhD, I bowed out after three years, master's degree in tow.

Once I left the PhD program, I realized that I still wanted to learn about brain function but from a more "human" experience. I wanted to learn about the function versus perception. In the world of psychiatry, understanding how people perceive their environment is critical. I tried to place myself in the patient's perspective. A person who struggles with hallucinations, delusions, or skewed perceptions experiences these perceptions as reality and needs to be treated with respect to their reality, while also being helped to maximize their functionality in the day-to-day world.

These individuals struggle every moment of every day with internal stimulus. This would be torture to an individual without these afflictions. In fact, a common torture method is to play music or a video at a loud volume and on a continuous loop so it cannot be ignored. People who struggle with internal stimuli have learned how to manage them and be functional to a degree. Functionality is based on the degree of the stimulus, the person's ability to cope with adversity, and his or her intelligence level. Some people who have severe internal stimuli and are incredibly intelligent learn how to perform remarkably well despite themselves, such as mathematician John Nash, whose biopic is *A Beautiful Mind*.

Psychiatry has come a long way in the treatment of people who struggle with mental disorders, but the general public still has a lot to learn. There are now programs to educate law enforcement and the legal system in how to better understand these behaviors and to work with them versus just reacting to them. I'm not advocating lenience, just understanding, so that we can work with these individuals and help them appropriately.

While working with this population, I got a clearer understanding of the term *crazy*. The definition of this term refers to derangement or insanity. These terms refer to acting out of the norm for the individual. We have come to misuse this term and turn it into a label.

I use the term *crazy* in its truest form: "perception/action out of the norm." My "crazy" is a state of mind in reaction to circumstances that I find baffling. I feel crazy when I cannot make sense of an action I have witnessed or heard about; I can't relate to it and yet I want to make sense of it. It's frustrating and I feel crazy. But thankfully, my constitution is such that I can still function and operate in the world. People who feel this way and are internally stimulated are not so fortunate.

So why all this talk about *crazy*? I think we have all felt crazy or acted crazy at least once in our lives, but instead judging it negatively, I challenge you to understand it. In the process of understanding you will know yourself better, understand others better, and may be entertained by some stories along the way.

Should you write your story down? Absolutely! Research has shown that our brains process information differently when we physically write something on paper. The mechanical function of writing with the creative process of storytelling allows the left and right brains to work together, producing an integrative process that allows for insight one might not otherwise experience.

Should you publish? Well, that is a question for an objective party: someone who can read your story and tell you if others would benefit.

For now…buckle up and join me on the ride of my life: *Front Row Seats to Crazy*.

CHAPTER 1

Owning a Carved Elephant Tusk Doesn't Make Me an Elephant Killer

I LOVE ELEPHANTS. NOT JUST because baby elephants are some of the cutest baby animals ever. No, no, this is not debatable.

I love elephants because they have an incredible sense of family. They do everything together and yet are unplagued by internal squabbles, like we humans suffer from in our own families. Elephants play, care for one another, protect their young and weak, work together to forage for food, birth their young together, and mourn their dead. There is an incredible story about a herd of elephants that made a two-day journey to visit the home of a man who had spent twenty years studying their behavior. When he passed away, they came to pay their respects.[1]

---

1 Lawrence Anthony, a legend in South Africa and author of three books, including the best-seller *The Elephant Whisperer*, bravely rescued wildlife and rehabilitated elephants all over the globe from human atrocities, including the courageous rescue of Baghdad Zoo animals during US invasion in 2003. On March 7, 2012, Lawrence Anthony died. He is remembered and missed by his wife, two sons, two grandsons, and numerous elephants. Two days after his passing, the wild elephants showed up at his home led by two large matriarchs. Separate wild herds arrived in droves to say goodbye to their beloved man-friend. A total of twenty elephants had patiently walked more than twelve miles to get to his South African house.

Witnessing this spectacle, humans were obviously in awe, not only because of the supreme intelligence and precise timing that these elephants sensed about Lawrence's passing but also because of the profound memory and emotion the beloved animals evoked in such an organized way: walking slowly—for days—making their way in a solemn one-by-one queue from their habitat to his house.

Lawrence's wife, François, was especially touched, knowing that the elephants had not been to his house prior to that day for well over a year! Yet they knew where they were going. The elephants obviously wanted to pay their deep respects, honoring their friend who'd saved their lives, so much respect that they stayed for two days and two nights. Then one morning they left, making their long journey back home.

My paternal grandfather was a medical missionary in central Africa. He lived and worked with the villagers of Sanga to create buildings that would later serve as their hospital and meeting halls. He spent twenty six years of his life with those villagers and in time he received many gifts of thanks for his help. Several of these gifts were made of ivory. Africans have long respected the power and love elephants embody. To give a gift of ivory is to recognize that spirit in another. I would love to tell you the ivory was only taken from old elephants that passed away from natural causes, but I don't know the truth. What I do know is the hand-carved ivory was given out of love and respect and it is with love and respect that I keep it.

I inherited the ivory from my father, who died much too young from cancer and maybe a broken heart. My father grew up in Sanga and had many fond memories of working with the villagers, helping his father in the hospital, and playing with his siblings out in the bush. I grew up watching eight-millimeter films and slides of villagers coming to visit my grandfather. They traveled for days and weeks while holding themselves up in precarious positions as they carried awkward goiters the size of basketballs on their necks and shoulders. Goiters of this type are commonly caused by a lack of iodine in your diet. They came from far and wide because they heard that Bwana Munanga, lord husband, would be able to heal them.

In truth, my grandfather was a great problem solver and loved the challenge these goiters presented to him. So at many family post-Thanksgiving and Christmas dinners, my cousins and I would sit in front of the projector as we watched villagers with gigantic goiters and big smiling faces go into the hospital for surgery. A week later they came back for their post-op appointment holding the goiter with an even bigger smile on their face and boasting of their new pink scar. Their whole demeanor had changed. Grandpa would also perform other medical procedures: fixing broken bones, treating illnesses, anything from basic care to intense surgery. He was the only Western medical practitioner in the area.

With a name like "lord husband" and a history of being a miraculous healer my grandfather never stood a chance of having a normal ego. He was, in fact, one of the most important men in the area, and everyone knew it.

My father was the middle child of five. The middle child is the hidden child. Often quiet and reserved, they watch others to determine the best course of action and are used to being overlooked. My father was named after the famous explorer Stanley Livingston. Livingston, too, was a quiet observer, but his love for adventure helped push him to become a renowned explorer. Like Livingston, my father loved the outdoors and wildlife. He earned his African name (Kitadi Kantanda, the governor of the country) while hunting a twenty-foot python; the skin was his reward. I now own the skin. It's rolled up next to the ivory tusk.

The names given to the men of my family by local villagers speak to the presence they had, an air about them. For my grandfather it was arrogance; for my father it was quiet observation—the ultimate middle child-ness. But there is something to be said for living in the middle of central Africa in the 1940s and 1950s. These were not easy times. Many things they had to learn to do without and many things they did not miss.

My grandmother missed her friends. Although she helped her husband out in the hospital as a nurse and cared for the family it was a lonely life. My father had siblings to play with but often found himself spending time with his mother. They were kindred spirits. The oldest siblings were close in age, adventurous, and daring, according to my father. They enjoyed hunting and fishing, enjoyed hearing stories and learning about the nature around them. They would all recognize what they were missing when they returned to the United States to take a break or get new commissions to be able to return to the mission. They all made sacrifices for the good of others. Those sacrifices formed who each of them were as people and who they were collectively as a family.

At the same time, a world away, my mother was raised in Sweden as a pastor's daughter. The eldest of two, she spent her childhood first in Stockholm, then a smaller town in the western part of Sweden, and then in the country... living the idyllic life of a Swedish girl. Being the eldest, she was the champion of the family, the first to strike out and seek adventure. She was a rebel, dyeing her hair at a young age, entering local theater productions, and adjusting her ensembles to reflect current fashion. She drew attention to herself, and this was not what a pastor's daughter was supposed to do. She got into trouble with her parents...a lot.

My parents met in England, at a small private college. My father went there because his uncle was the dean and he was expected to be near family.

My mother went there because it was the farthest she could go to school while working on her English-speaking skills. Their college years include some fun stories I will tell later, but for now I will say it was love at first sight. They were together for fifty years through all life's challenges.

It is their story that inspired me to write this book. But I realized their story is not really mine to tell. So I will tell my story, because by telling it I have learned a lot about myself and my parents. The stories I have gathered over the years are inspired by the amazing people in my life.

Both my parents left lasting impressions on nearly everyone they met. As their only child, I am left with their legacies: my mother, the troublemaker, and my father, the quiet observer.

However, I discovered in the telling of their stories that my father could also be a troublemaker and my mother a quiet observer.

So perhaps my legacy will be how I survived them and what I learned along the way.

CHAPTER 2

The Exception to the Rule

Now I'm about to say something that is highly controversial.

It is OK to judge. In fact, it is necessary for our survival. The definition of *judgment* is "the ability to make considered decisions or come to sensible conclusions." How do we make considered decisions?

We take in information using our various senses. The information is then paired with similar information in our cerebral cortex, and the pairings allow for associations with other experiences and memories. These comparisons allow us to consider how this new information compares to what is already known to our experiences and we judge how to respond. This process can happen very quickly or take more time depending on the person and his or her level of personal awareness.

Our first impressions are a result of judgment. We then continue to have a choice about how we respond to our judgments. A person who is self-aware may acknowledge a first impression as unhealthy or incomplete and may reserve judgment until more information is gathered. This practice is also adopted by many Eastern philosophies advocating meditation and reflection prior to action. This can be as simple as a deep breath or as complicated as taking time away from our daily life to meditate and reflect on experiences to discern the "correct" course of action.

Based on the information given above, judgment is not negative. However, when I say it's OK to judge...you will still likely cringe at this statement. We are conditioned through societal norms to be open and affirming, to listen and accept people for who they are and what they believe in; everyone's experience is unique and considered valuable in its own right.

So, how do we reconcile the survival instinct and reality of daily judgment with societal norms and expectations of acceptance? Most of the time we continue on in private, sometimes unconscious judgment and create an outward persona who is encouraging and accepting while inwardly we hold grudges and fixate on negative impressions. When we do decide to create a boundary through a judgment, then we must be willing to defend the judgment; this can encourage a determination to hold the line despite new information that would otherwise provide a different perspective. This can lead to negative labels and further stubbornness.

If, instead of digging in our heels, we remain educated on our positions and willing to discuss our point of view with the opportunity to consider new information, then we have the opportunity for personal growth. This requires a great deal more work mentally, physically, and spiritually.

So we opt for the quick solution: first impressions are lasting impressions. I'm an only child.

Right now you are having a reaction…dare I say a judgment?

Only children are typically considered spoiled, entitled, selfish, unwilling to share…the list goes on.

I am Caucasian. My parents were both highly educated. They were born outside of the country and educated in Europe. Our family home was located on one of the oldest golf courses in Southern California. I love horses and had them in my life from the time I was six years old.

So now that you have vilified me as a part of the 1 percent who oppresses the rest of the world with my existence, consider this…

I graduated from a liberal college. My senior thesis was about how to help encourage people to have protected sex for the purpose of preventing sexually transmitted diseases. I taught high school science and got in trouble with several parents for teaching sex education, including how to use condoms, and showing the film *And the Band Played On*, a film on the beginnings of AIDS in the country and gay male culture. I'm fiscally conservative but support gay rights. I lived with a friend in a mobile home park for a few months.

I'm not trying to win you over, just providing more information that might give you an opportunity to consider that basic demographics do not always mean what you assume.

Most of the time when people take the time to get to know me they will comment that I am not the typical only child and they are surprised to hear I am one!

My challenge to you is to consider who in your life is really the exception to the rule?

How do people view you?

Are you the exception or the rule?

Maybe you have your own "elephant tusk" at home and worry about who might judge you for owning it.

Here's the next shocking thing I'm going to say: my mother was a judgmental person.

I watched my mother, an intelligent, culturally aware individual fall over herself emotionally rushing to make judgments. Once I got past the initial reaction...which took decades on my part, I figured out what the drive behind the judgments was: fear.

We fear what we don't understand or relate to or what we feel challenged by. These are our survival instincts: our fight-or-flight response, our primal selves telling us how to survive. The last shocking thing I will say is this: you cannot make anyone feel something.

We feel our feelings in response to our perceptions. Our perceptions are based on our experiences combined with the physical sensations we experience, and how we process the combination is unique to each of us. It is why you can get ten different accounts of the same event by ten different witnesses.

A person's feelings are theirs, initiated as a response to the physical environment they find themselves in and the internal environment they experience based on their understanding of what is happening: their perceptions.

Our judgements are a reflection of our perceptions. We judge whether something is safe to touch based on received temperature, texture, and surroundings. We judge whether it is safe to trust someone based on their physical appearance, their body language, and the circumstance we are in.

Judgments are meant to keep us safe. Judgments become destructive when we make assumptions without considering new information—when we become complacent and react to our past knowledge versus working to understand the current circumstance. This requires engagement, connection, opportunity for personal growth, and potential challenge to past understanding. Challenge can create uncertainty. Uncertainty can illicit anxiety. Anxiety can lead to fear. Fear triggers the fight-or-flight response, and, just like that, we are back to our primal selves: making judgments to survive.

So the real question is, are you working to survive life or live it? Are you willing to take each opportunity as a learning opportunity, which may prove to strengthen previous associations or challenge them? This is not a question I ask lightly. I hope you will strongly consider having a life filled with questions and challenges to your personal understanding of the world. It is a riskier life but I believe a more interesting one to live.

CHAPTER 3

Nature vs. Nurture

I WAS A QUIET CHILD by all reports. I think some innate part of me knew not to rock the boat. I slept through the night very early on in my infancy to the point that my mother was convinced I would die of SIDS and checked on me regularly.

I remember being very small and watching other children getting angry, throwing tantrums, or even talking back to their parents. I felt shocked and a bit afraid about what was going to happen to them for such outrageous behavior. So, was this innate knowledge or imposed by outside stimuli? Did my parents give me a look, use a tone or certain body language to train me to have these thoughts? Probably both, but which influenced me more…the nature or the nurture?

Regardless of which I was responding to, I knew acting out would have serious consequences that I did not want to experience. I am not accusing my parents of abuse. I know that did not happen. However, I will say there was something intangible I feared about my parents. Something I unconsciously responded to for years.

In my late teens, I discovered that my mother's only sibling had waited until he was three before he walked and talked. The first three years of his life he sat and watched the world go by, often smiling or softly giggling, rarely upset. My mother, who was five years his senior, thought he was an idiot… literally. This judgment of idiocy would turn out to be a theme in my mother's life directed at anyone she didn't understand or relate to. My mother claimed she never thought I was an idiot but she never understood me either, a dynamic that was established early in our relationship.

As a quiet child, I was relatively easy to deal with while out running errands. My mother would make sure I had something to do in the form of a toy, coloring book, or, in the early years, my blanket to hold. I did not like pacifiers but preferred the middle and ring finger of my left hand. I often wonder if this wasn't my own unconscious speaking out as a big eff you to the world I found myself in but rarely understood.

When I was eighteen months old on an errand with my mother at a local retail store that sold everything under the sun, I made a noise, not just any noise, mind you, a squeal of excitement and pointed at the object I desired. Up to this point in my short life, this had never happened…ever. So what was so important?

On the shelf across and out of my reach stood a row of plastic horses, which I can now say were Breyer horses. I was pointing to one in particular. When my mother reached for the horse next to the one I wanted I shook my head and pointed earnestly to the one I wanted. She took it from the shelf and handed it to me. Apparently, I was in awe and held it on my lap for the rest of the errand, the ride home post-purchase (just in case you imagined my mother and me making a run for it with toy horse in tow), and the rest of the night. That is when they discovered my love of horses, and I have never lived without one since.

But why that horse? What was so special about that model that no other one would do? Why horses at all for that matter? We lived in the city, no horses around, no family with horses, no friends with horses, no genetic connection except for one relative on my father's side. My great-great-grandmother loved horses and famously rode hers up the courthouse steps somewhere in Tennessee. I even have a picture of her on her horse in full nineteenth-century riding habit—very regal. But aside from this remote connection, there was no explaining my affection for horses.

However, once Pandora's box was opened, I could not get enough. I loved pictures, toys, books… anything horse. My father took me to Western Town, an old west theme park complete with all the "attractions" of life in the late 1800's, to see a horse while I was still in diapers. How do I know this? Because I have a picture of myself sitting on a stuffed horse in a bucking position with a huge grin on my face, pantaloons displayed for everyone to see. Literally, this will be a theme in my life...always showing my underwear.

I did get to ride live ponies as well and have many pictures of myself, from the age of two on, smiling, squinting in the sun while my pony walks the narrow path built for him to follow.

I loved Western Town and consequently spoke up whenever a pony ride presented itself. This was back in the 1970s, when things like lawsuits for riding ponies in a parking lot of a grocery store or outside the mall were not even a twinkle in a person's eye. Instead, there was a decent-size tent with a small pipe-fenced arena and a mechanical walker with four ponies attached all evenly spaced and timed. It was a real live carousel and ruined me for wood-carved horse carousels. However, I didn't pass them up when offered a ride. I still feel an inward tug to a carousel when I see one.

When I first heard the story of the Breyer horse at the store and my reaction to it—the beginning of my lifelong love for horses and a large collection of horses—I immediately wanted to know which horse was my first horse. I showed my mother my collection, asking for a detailed description so she could select the horse from the crowd. Much to my frustration, she was never clear on the details. It was brownish, had a halter on its face; it was a "normal" size, not a small one; that part she was sure of. It was in a position of movement, not standing. At the time, I had a two that met the description. But according to my mother it was neither of them. How is this possible? I did not get rid of anything horse. Anything. Was it stolen? Did I leave it somewhere and not say anything? This I cannot imagine because as an only child I am very protective of my stuff and certainly don't just leave things around to be picked up by someone else.

So where is this horse?

I find myself on a quest. A quest on which the characters are already in play and will stay this way throughout the journey: my mother, who was present but fuzzy on the details, my father who facilitated happy moments but also encouraged my vulnerability. Horses that gave me a voice and helped me identify what I wanted and needed in life, a quiet reflection, which has connected me to everything around me for better and for worse.

Questing

A quest is often seen as a noble cause. Inviting images of knights, damsels in distress, villages in need of saving, causes to be won. But a quest can also evoke memories of Don Quixote, the search for the Holy Grail, and perhaps, in current times, peace and justice for all. So, was my quest one of futility or meaning? It started with a need to place "my first horse" in a space of special honor and turned into an ongoing desire to get to the truth, to fill in the blanks, to understand.

Not everyone takes on quests. In fact, few do. Most are interested by the stories, perhaps living vicariously through the experience. Some will be inspired to seek out their own quest, but most will express a basic curiosity about the story and then, having heard it once, move on to other things. So, is the need to quest nature or nurture? Given the previous statements, I would argue it is nature. But I like to research things (quest), so I looked it up.

It turns out there's a gene for that: DRD4 r7, a rare gene, located in only 20 percent of the general population. People who exhibit this gene are explorers of people, places, and things. They are social and enjoy new things, can be risk takers and are often identified as restless. Sixty-six percent of the population age ninety years and above have this gene. Do they live longer because they are involved in life, or does their genetic predisposition encourage a long life? They do tend to appreciate life, enjoying the small things, if you will. The researcher (Grady) suggests more research needs to be done but identified some interesting patterns. The bibliographic information for his research is: Grady DL et al. 2013. DRD4 Genotype Predicts Longevity in Mouse and Human. *The Journal of Neuroscience*, 33 (1): 286-291; doi: 10.1523/ JNEUROSCI.3515-12.2013

I certainly come from a family of adventurers. Most lived into their late eighties and nineties. My parents did not, but they were risk takers and loved to travel. So perhaps my questing, my need to know, is genetically predisposed.

Then why the huge disconnect between my mother and myself? As two questers, we should have been able to relate to each other. I think this confused her too, but we never really did understand our differences and it took longer than life itself to resolve or come to peace with our disconnect. That story will come later.

For now we will return to the horse. My first pony was a loaner from a colleague of my father whose daughter was in pony club. I learned the basics of horse husbandry, care of equipment, and riding from pony club. Two ponies later, I moved on to quarter horses. This came about through an unfortunate but all too familiar episode, of my pony telling me how things were going to be, witnessed by the local quarter horse trainer, who had helped me and my pony through our most recent debacle and then introduced me to a quieter, more symbiotic relationship with a quarter horse.

My parents had their own reasons for introducing me, I'm sure, since they were willing to let me show: this would turn out to be a lucrative deal for them. But it was also a meaningful experience for me. All told I competed through my preadolescent and adolescent years. I traveled throughout the state of California and I was both regionally and nationally competitive. I rode horses every day after school and only started playing sports my sophomore year of high school. Juggling riding, school, and sports kept me out of the trouble, I'm convinced I would have been in if I hadn't been otherwise occupied.

Now, given my previous stories, you might be led to believe it was my father who took me riding and accompanied me to the shows, but it was actually my mother. We were gone thirty to forty weekends of the year for four years in a row. A typical quarter horse show schedule often started at six in the morning and I didn't go to bed until eleven o'clock at night. My friends were on the show circuit with me, although I had a few in school. It was tough to keep up with my friendships with such a grueling schedule. Few outside the routine could keep up. I was surprised my mother kept up. I often waited for both my parents to pull the plug and tell me I needed to change my focus. So this just drove me harder to succeed. If I was a champion they would let me continue.

I won more than thirty regional and local year-end championships and several national awards over a span of seven years. I was fortunate with many of the horses I rode, but not all were competitive in the show ring. I learned how to lose gracefully and cry in the privacy of my own tack room or trailer when defeat really challenged me. I learned how personal prejudice can change the course of your life and goals if you let it and how you have to find value in the doing of a thing, not the result. OK, the last one took a really long time to learn, and I still glean insights into this layered process as life goes on.

I could easily recount stories for each horse I have had in my life and their meaning to me, but that is not the point of this journey and I am attempting to keep us on track.

CHAPTER 4

Frozen—Not the Disney Story

THE FIRST TIME I FROZE…TIME slowed down.

My mother was with me and we were in the house I grew up in moving from upstairs to downstairs. I remember feeling a lot of tension, but whatever had caused the tension had passed. I was relieved but then I just slowed down, like I was moving in slow motion. I knew nothing had changed physically around me, yet I felt slow, disconnected from my environment. I was still physically moving and processing at the same rate, but something else was not. My body felt suspended, unable to respond at a normal rate. This state did not last long, and when I felt I was able, I asked my mother if she noticed anything different about me. She said no. She didn't understand, and I knew I couldn't explain what had just happened.

This is, in fact, a form of a fugue state: a brief disconnection to current circumstances through a feeling of slowed time, occasionally portrayed in war films by soldiers in the heat of battle. It is a response to trauma, to keep a person moving despite outside stimulus to the contrary. In battle this response make sense. In a home environment …

What did I witness? Does it really matter?

I don't think so. I think what matters is how I managed this "condition." This "condition" is debilitating for some people who have been exposed to trauma to the degree that they are unable to "snap out of it." The degree of the trauma exposure is variable for every person and their personal mental constitution. For example, some soldiers returning from deployment will appear OK and able to integrate with their family nearly immediately, but some struggle to reconnect. For those who do reconnect and then go on multiple deployments, it can be that over time that they are not able to reconnect or their struggle with reconnection increases over time.

How is it there is so much variability in this reaction?

Welcome to our amazingly unique brains/psyches.

In my case, I have gone most my life "white-knuckling" these moments. They are rare, and when they occur I acknowledge them but don't take time to process them at all. Now, having survived multiple life changes and stressors (both uncontrolled and intentional), I have come to the realization that life is too valuable to not challenge myself to be the best that I can be, which, in my case, means that looking at things I have acknowledged but never processed is not acceptable. Acknowledgment is not understanding.

It is time to thaw.

The theme song from the Disney movie *Frozen* became a hit sensation almost overnight. Kids around the world just couldn't get enough of it. There is something to the idea of "just let it go…" However, if you don't properly thaw and learn from your behaviors, you will never learn, and letting go won't be an option. Thawing is an important process. But if done incorrectly, one can get burned or can rot.

This writing project is my version of thawing. It's a multilayered process. I spent the first year dumping thoughts onto paper, the next year gathering resources and further reflecting, the next processing previously learned information through my formal education and therapy work, and finally bringing to my exploration exposure to my reflections. In the safety of close friends and family, I shared my thoughts and dreams and reflections of life and decided it was time to let go of the past ghosts and move into acceptance of my future. The rest of this story will be reflective layers, the glacier of my life slowly melting into the sea of my future…

CHAPTER 5

Intellectual Powerhouses

LET'S START AT THE BEGINNING because I hear it's a very good place to start. (If you start humming a song from *The Sound of Music* I won't tell anyone.)

My beginning. Why the distinction? I have been asked to tell my story on multiple occasions. I came to realize that my pattern is to start with my parents and their upbringing. I felt and still do that my parent's beginnings influence who we were as a family. Since I am the sole survivor of the family, their stories will now forever be a part of my story. As a therapist with a psychodynamics inclination, I understand how the developmental process of our parents influences their children's lives by passing on their own experiences into their parenting style and relational style. Only through intense concentration and active engagement do we break the patterns of our family upbringing. This explains generational behavior and adds to the complexity of the nature-versus-nurture discussion. But it is all from the adult perspective. Somehow, even as a child, I knew my parents were acting out their family stuff within our family of three.

When I first started this writing project I planned to write my story and then write my parents' stories. However, I have since realized that their opportunity to tell their stories has passed. Any story I write will be from my perspective, so I will include their stories as a part of this book distinguishing it from my own when it's not painfully obvious.

My story involves them for obvious reasons but it was the sudden one-two punch of my parents dying that drove me to want to understand this latest bit of crazy. I have always felt the need to make sense of crazy. One could argue, this need is what drove me to become a therapist in the first place.

When was the first time I felt crazy? I'd say as a late toddler when my mother started to pull away from me emotionally.

I started grieving for my mother long before she actually passed away.

You see, in the therapy world, in order to move through a problem you must understand first what it is that you want. What is the reality? And can you bridge the two…wanting vs. reality? Inevitably, you will find that you must grieve some part of what you want, just let it go, to find the workable solution.

My mother and I were not suited for each other.

Please don't misunderstand me. We loved each other but we were a mismatched set almost from the start. It seems odd to me that in the day of "I am individual; hear me roar" so much of who we are is credited to our parents. General consensus is that if you are not like one, then you must be like the other. Rarely are comparisons made to an aunt or uncle; however, there is the occasional grandparent reference. Now, of course, I understand, perhaps better than most, how we are products of our environments both genetically and in the behaviors we exhibit; certainly, there is a lot I have in common with my parents. However, much to my chagrin, I found them to be people I could not relate to in the most fundamental ways.

I was raised to respect my elders, speak when spoken to, mind my manners, and be patient. Unlike most children I observe today, my early childhood was about my parents' lives, not mine. My father enjoyed taking me for pony rides when I was young, and my mother invested time in my equestrian career while I was an adolescent. But I followed them, not the other way around.

According to close family accounts, my mother was very concerned about doing things right with me when I was born. She turned to her reliable resource: books. She read the current experts on child-rearing and through cross-referencing the most popular books with the most recent she determined her plan. I'm sure she received advice from her parents and in-laws, but in later years when the subject came up it was the books she referenced.

So I had a schedule for sleep, food, changing, and playtime. As the only child and one of few kids in our little group of friends, I had little to compare to, but something told me at a very young age, I'd better fall in line or else. I wouldn't challenge this concept until much, much later in life.

When my mother went out, I went with her. I had a small bag of toys to keep me entertained, and that suited me just fine. When I was at home I played in my room or outside. I didn't play with my mother, not because she wasn't interested; it just never came up. She was busy doing her thing—reading books, watching a political show on TV, or talking to friends on the phone—and I was busy doing my thing. My father was busy with his medical school residency and then studying for the boards. When he took a break from all that, he was outside in the garden. Often we were outside together but rarely doing the same thing.

I spent time with my parents separately, not intentionally, again; it's just what happened. I followed my mother's schedule during the week and my father's schedule on the weekends.

I loved the weekends because they meant adventure. My father and I would start with going to the hospital to complete his patient rounds (I sat at the nurses' station with my bag of toys), then we would go about our errands, which always included some form of farm-related activity like getting chickens, food for the animals, stuff for the tractor...and hamburgers for lunch. At least once a month, we went to Western Town. I would get several pony rides on ponies that followed one another on a little track. I didn't care about the restrictions; I was happy to be riding. I loved everything about it: the smell of the pony, the clopping sound of the hooves, the wind in my hair. OK, that's a stretch, but you get the point. I was truly happy when I rode a pony.

Then we would wander "the town," share a snack, and head home. Other times we would work in the yard, go to the local feed store for chicken feed, select chicks that would later become the chickens that produced different colored eggs. (Who says you always have to color your eggs for Easter? I just went and got mine from the coop!) The chore of picking up the eggs would become my morning task before school. These tasks of caring for and spending time with animals gave me purpose, and I loved every minute of it. They were also made possible by my father, who paid for these adventures and encouraged my animal husbandry activities.

I have a great story I've told many times about my father and our rooster Charlie.

The Charlie Story

Because it was my morning chore to pick up the eggs, I became very familiar with the sounds and behaviors of our chickens. The chicken coop was located at the bottom of our property right next to the golf course. This was lovely for the golfer who paid a lot of money to golf on this course and could hear our chickens, specifically Charlie, early in the morning. The course was located in a canyon that had wonderful acoustics, and Charlie loved to try them out. Our neighbors were not amused and threatened to have Charlie removed, so my father came up with a solution.

One morning I came down to collect eggs and I noticed the chickens were very quiet and not visible. Normally, I could hear them making their soft cooing noises and see them in their fenced yard scratching the for grubs and food. But not today. Today they were hiding in the coop and barely making a peep. When I rounded the corner to the gate of the coop I discovered why.

My father, the surgeon, had prepped a surgical area right in the middle of the coop, using sawhorses and plywood for a surgery table complete with surgical drapes from a hospital and his patient on the table: Charlie.

Dad was wearing scrubs, complete with head cover and mask—in a chicken coop!

I took this all in in a matter of moments before he looked up at me, from his patient, placed a gloved finger across his mask and whispered "Shh. Don't tell your mother." I promptly ran back up to the house and told my mother. She just rolled her eyes and told me not to worry about it; there was nothing we could do now and Charlie would likely be OK.

Charlie did survive the surgery, which was meant to cut his vocal chords so that the neighbors would be happy. Charlie was not happy and proceeded with physical therapy immediately. It took several months but sure enough he got his crow back. Charlie underwent the surgery two more times after the first unsuccessful attempt. The second had similar results to the first, and the third was a near miss. On this occasion Dad noticed that Charlie had become particularly cooperative during surgery and Dad was really pleased with how things were going until he considered checking on his patient, at which time he found that Charlie's comb was turning blue and dad needed to give him mouth-to-beak resuscitation. He brought him back and admitted that he was not a veterinarian, so perhaps he should just leave Charlie's crow alone. Charlie lived out the rest of his days with his flock, crowing his scratchy crow to his heart's content.

My mother was an enigma to me. She was otherworldly, untouchable, unreachable. As a child I would watch her and tell her stories of the things I saw around me to capture her attention. As I grew older, I found myself struggling to relate to her. She was poised in her dress and demeanor. When she spoke to friends she was on fire with her most recent intellectual musing on current political affairs, world history, and religious/cultural beliefs. Inevitably, something outraged her during these conversations and she would lecture with such ferocity, it was a sight to behold or listen to…which one could easily do within 200 feet of said conversation. To say that my mother was passionate would be an understatement. In order to truly enjoy her passion you had to be in line with it or you would need to defend the reasons why you had other ideas. "Because" and "I don't think so," were unacceptable and quickly dismissed as "idiotic." *Know your mind or don't bother me with your argument* was my mother's mantra.

As a defense for my mother's idiosyncratic line of reasoning, I tapped into my genetic heritage of stubbornness: adopt a stance in any discussion and hold on to it…no matter what. I became a talented debater. In simpler times this was an amazing skill and one that earned me a reputation of championing causes others would not dare buck the system to champion. However, the negative side was that I held onto fleeting thoughts with just as much ferocity, unable to see that they were just stepping stones to bigger, more important ideas. This has derailed my life several times, much to my and my mother's frustration.

I'm a daydreamer, always have been, and it used to get me in a lot of trouble. I would like to think I have corralled this into creative thinking and writing, but the jury is still out.

THE PARENT–TEACHER CONFERENCE

When I was in kindergarten, I got in trouble for staring out the window instead of looking at the teacher when she was talking. My mother was called in for a parent–teacher conference and informed of the problem. My mother's response? "Well, Ms. ——, if you would just be more interesting, I'm sure this would no longer be a problem." Ms. —— was dumbfounded and had nothing else to say, furthering my mother's point, so we left. Needless to say, there were no more parent–teacher conferences for the next six years at that school. When I got in trouble my mother was not informed lest they experience her wrath.

As I have already illustrated, my father and I were more like-minded in how we spent our time together. We liked to do things together. My father came from a long line of "doers," but more on this later. I enjoyed spending time with my dad because we naturally got along since we both liked to be active and outdoors. When I was very young, my father and I were simpatico. As I grew older, my father and I would butt heads about what things we liked to do. I liked to go skiing for an hour or two, he preferred to go all day. His logic was sound: since the cost of a ski lift ticket was almost the same, why not go for the whole day? The problem with this idea for me was that then it became a chore…ski, ski, ski, grab a quick bite to eat, and go, go, go. I felt wasteful if I didn't ski the entire time. This idea of being wasteful, in terms of how money is spent, will be a major bone of contention for both my parents and me throughout our lives together. My mother, on the other hand, could drift down the hill at her own pace for an hour or two, then she would take an extended break, and then repeat. This worked for her but frustrated my father but he dared not say anything to her, so it was left up to me to ski with Dad. No bag of toys to save me.

From the time I was six, my mother and I would spend at least a month of my summer vacation in Sweden. My dad would come for about two weeks. This happened three years in a row, and then my riding career interrupted the plan. At least that is what I was told. I suspect otherwise now.

When I was seven, my father received an internship in England and we lived in London for about six months. My parents brought my Great-Aunt Helen as my nanny. Her sense of adventure made everything we did together fun. She loved to explore and we had many adventures together. I remember having fun on our first few trips to Europe.

THE CINDERELLA OPERA STORY

Because I grew up in Southern California, Disneyland was a reality for me. I was intimately familiar with all the Disney stories and characters. So when my parents and I went to an opera in Vienna (one guess whose idea this was...) featuring the Cinderella story, I had certain expectations.

We had excellent seats, of course, since my mother had planned the excursion: third row, center stage—dead center. The music began, the curtain rose, and soon Cinderella appeared. In this case, Cinderella was portrayed by a typical opera singer, who did not appear as Disney had portrayed Cinderella.

Now, she was singing center stage and I got the giggles. I was literally shaking with hysterics; my father who knew immediately why I was laughing started to giggle too. We are now in serious trouble. The singer realized that we were laughing at her!

We have all been there. You start giggling, then a person with you starts, and now neither one of you can stop and it becomes this infectious thing that just has to play itself out.

This is where my father and I found ourselves. My mother was horrified. Cinderella was singing and staring right at us, which only made us laugh harder because her face was turning purple with anger. My father and I were inconsolable, and then it happened. A theater employee came to our row and asked us to step out until we could pull ourselves together. My father and I stepped out, my mother was furious, and I think we left because I can't remember the rest of the play.

As a child, let's say before the age of ten, I felt more comfortable with my father. He was willing to do things I wanted to do and seemed to enjoy them.

Having said that, my mother started to get involved in my horse/pony affection when I started pony club at the age of seven. She hauled me out to the barn at least four days a week and took me to shows. This amazed me, and I am forever grateful that she facilitated this part of my life. My mother and I spent more time together once I became more involved with horses. At this point in my life it was my mother and I who spent the majority of our time together and my father became more remote. It wasn't easy for him to go to the horse shows since he was on call every other weekend and the shows would often start on a Friday. I missed school on those Fridays and took my schoolwork with me. I was able to keep up my grades, and my mother, well, my school did not really have much of a choice in this matter.

As I grew older, barn life was a real comfort to me. However, spending this much time with my mother had its strains. This was not her element; she did not ride and found the people who did friendly but not intellectually stimulating. So she was bored, but miraculously she hung in there for six years. On my sixteenth birthday, I got my driver's license and my freedom. I maintained my riding/training schedule for a year but became more involved with school and college prep in the last year and a half of high school. After I graduated, I took a break from competing horses.

Throughout high school, my parents and I would take vacations on my school breaks. Winter break was a ski trip to Utah or Colorado, and spring break was Hawaii. These were always great places to visit and explore, yet I don't remember them fondly. At this point, my family was made up of three individuals who were more like roommates than a family. I remember a lot of tension between my parents. My father wanted to explore and be outside and my mother wanted to wander, read, and relax. I was torn between wanting to do a little of both yet feeling like I was choosing sides if I did either. I disliked the tension. I tried to avoid the tension by spending time with one of them but then I would feel guilty. So I have all these beautiful pictures of these vacations, and yet when you look at us, there is obvious tension. It's sad we couldn't figure out what was happening at the time and work out a way to compromise so that we really could do all the things we wanted to do and enjoy each other. This is a theme I found all too familiar as my life continued.

Competing horses gave me a purpose and an outlet for my teenage angst, but it also became a financial concern since it is so expensive. When it comes to money, my mother and father could not be further apart in their belief systems, and I am somewhere in the middle. My mother believed in real estate investments and buying a small amount of good-quality verses a bunch of poorer quality items. She had excellent taste and was known for it among all who knew her. My father treated money like it was a hot potato. If you asked him what his financial belief system was he would tell you once you take care of your responsibilities then you should share with others and, of course, invest. He struggled with follow-through in this department, however. He wasn't comfortable with financial planning or budgeting. He blamed some of this on my mother, who liked to shop for good-quality things.

Bottom line, they fought about finances and rarely agreed on financial questions/concerns. The result: as a neurosurgeon in the 1980s my father made enough money that my parents could spend it without discussion or real discretion. My father made several poor investments; in fact, I don't think he ever invested in a successful venture until his last business. My mother's reaction to his poor choices was to buy amazing things for the house; invest in my riding career, which amounted to more horses, trainers, and larger competitions; and not worry about where the money came from, except she did… she worried about it all the time.

So by the time I was fifteen, I, in my infinite wisdom, started to chime in to solve the financial concerns of my parents with statements like, "Hey, folks, let's not buy more horses, or we could sell some of the ones we have. How about instead of buying jewelry, you sell some. Maybe we shouldn't go on a trip if money is tight?"

Now, on the surface, these comments could be seen as logical, even obvious, but instead they enraged my mother. How dare, I, a fifteen-year-old, insist I have an answer, and I was apparently ungrateful for all my father did for me in the way of horses, competing, jewelry, clothes, and amazing vacations. The tirade would continue despite my trying to explain myself, which would only get me into a deeper hole, until my mother got tired and walked away, or I did.

I would love to tell you this only happened once or twice and then I learned my lesson. But, you forget, I'm stubborn and have to stick to a point once I've made it…especially one so reasonable. So this went on for years and years and years. When I was in my twenties, I started asking my parents about their financial plan. Do they have a will, a trust, a plan? Again came the tirade that always ended with…"Don't worry about it, little girl, you'll be taken care of when we die…you will get all this stuff!"

These discussions became a framework of tension between my parents and me. It hung over us anytime we were together and added a negative tint to anything we did together as a family. It was exhausting and never-ending. Even if the central topics were avoided, the anticipation of a fight was always there, so it was difficult for my parents to enjoy each other or me.

I moved away for college. Strange, I know.

I stayed close enough that I could go home on the weekends or my parents could come visit me, but far enough away to continue to establish my independence. I saw and heard from my parents less and less. My mother did come to visit several times my first year and I spoke to her on the phone a couple of times a week. I don't remember speaking to my father that often.

Since I was done competing horses and my parents still had the horse ranch they had purchased several years before, complete with fifteen of our own horses, I had an idea. I wanted to take responsibility for the ranch. I wanted to sell the horses so that they could continue with their various careers and be well cared for and so I could use the money to pay for my college tuition—solving another financial concern in my own way. But why stop there? If the ranch was no longer being used perhaps I could sell the equipment, the barns, fencing, and whatever else I could sell to pay for college. My parents agreed and that is exactly what I did. They paid for my first semester and I paid for the rest with the proceeds from the sales. This was a great business experience for me and a huge relief when it came to the ongoing family financial feud.

My senior year of college brought a new concern as I was worried about what my next step in life would be. I had lost major confidence in my original plan. I was pre- med with the intention of keeping up the family tradition of becoming a doctor. But that hadn't been my original plan. Like many children, I wanted to be a veterinarian. In high school I allowed myself the option of medical doctor since I was already worried that I didn't have the grades to get into vet school. When I got to college I found that the pre-vet students were really serious and very bright. I also discovered that because of this it was much more difficult to get into veterinarian school than medical school. I felt like I didn't stand a chance, so I just let it go and focused on med school. But even that slipped away as my interest waned.

This was in the early 1990s when medical insurance was changing and private clinicians were having a hard time adapting. My father was frustrated by this change in medicine and the financial consequences of the change only added fuel to our little family financial boulder hanging over all our heads.

After many discussions with my father, I decided not to go to medical school. I didn't even try. So now what would I do with myself?

To add to the confusion, two weeks after graduation I got into a terrible riding accident and ended up in the hospital for two days with a broken nose, a knot on my forehead, a third degree concussion, a huge tear on the inside of my bottom lip where my teeth almost went all the way through, and two hemorrhaged eyeballs. I was a mess. After a few weeks of recovery, I got back on my horse (not the one that had bucked me off) and started to face my life again.

I went to work for my dad in his office. Later that summer I started a teaching credential program. The following year I taught middle school and high school science. I found I enjoyed teaching but not the political dynamics needed to survive parents, other teachers, and the administrators. So I went to graduate school for my PhD in cognitive psychology. I left after three years with my MA instead.

In the meantime, my mother, who was managing my father's office (and had been since my second year of college), had to go to Sweden to visit her ailing father. He passed away soon after she got there and she was devastated. In fact, it changed her. She was so depressed and despondent, my temporary job of helping with the office while she was away became permanent.

I found myself managing my parents' finances. Finally, I could get things organized and solve the problems once and for all! Yeah, right...oh, the fantasies.

It is true, by the time my father retired in 2003, he was debt free and had a decent retirement account. I handed over the financial reins, and within three months the debts were safely back in place and I gave up the discussion.

In 2004, I successfully completed my second master of arts degrees in psychology. I had a job at a residential treatment center for women who struggle with chemical dependency. I had a great start to completing the three thousand hours of clinical time needed to apply for licensure. I owned a house with a community barn where I had one horse. I was newly married to my boyfriend of five and half years. My mother didn't like him; she thought he was a waste of my time and an insult to her as a parent. My father had his concerns but tried to be supportive.

BLOWOUT

December 28, 2004, my back blew out… technically, my L5-S1 disc wrapped around my nerve root, rendering me in terrible pain and unable to sit or walk without a major limp.

January 1, 2005, my father, the neurosurgeon, met me and my husband at the hospital where his main practice was once located. He ordered scans and discovered the problem. He told me the following: "I'm not sure you will ever be able to ride again [tears stream down my face]; you will not be able to drive for three months; you will not be able to sit comfortably for six months. In about eighteen months you might completely recover; I've seen it happen with younger people. Now it's time to get you in the pool."

For years I had listened to my father tell his patients that the best physical therapy for back problems was swimming. It's always good to work through positive resistance without the weight of your body pulling on your back; you can go at your own pace and chose a stroke that is the least painful. For years I would hear my father ask his patients, "Are you swimming?" and the patient would most often say, "No, doctor, but I know you recommend it."

So I swam for the first two weeks under his supervision, complete with a wide support belt often used for heavy lifting. I had one that I used for swimming and one that I wore the rest of the time. I even slept in it the first two weeks. I took hydrocodone for two weeks, I took a steroid for several months, and I swam almost every day.

I went back to work three days after my father's diagnosis. My mother drove me home from work a few times that first month, which amazed me every time and I was grateful each time. My father came to check on me at least once a week and we swam together. I had an amazing supervisor who lived close by and she volunteered to pick me up and take me home the other days. I am eternally grateful for her sacrifice and generosity. But all this painfully points out that my mother's suspicions about my husband where right. He did not help very much. At times, he made an effort but would soon become annoyed by my lack of ability to do much of anything besides go to work, come home, and rest.

If you have ever been in severe pain, then you understand what I mean when I say it's a game changer.

I had a whole new appreciation for what my clients faced on a daily basis. To their credit, they tolerated my working with them while I spent the first three months on my knees propped over an ottoman and then the next six months in an ergonomic chair in which your knees are below your waist at an angle, a gift from my father.

Every day was exhausting, and yet I was grateful to get out of the house, away from my sad marriage and escape into some else's pain. If I couldn't help myself, at least I could try to help these amazing women who really wanted to change their lives. They inspired me but I was sadly slow to change myself.

The adage "sometimes you have to burn your hand on the stove in order to learn it's hot" needs to be adapted in the case of my failed marriage, too. Sometimes you have to watch your hand go up in flames and put out the fire, repeat several times, and then you realize it's safer if you just leave the kitchen.

Over the next three long years I discovered the following things to be true. My father's predictions about my back and its recovery were exactly right. I started driving short distances three months later. I graduated to the abovementioned chair around the same time and a real chair at six months (for short periods of time). At eighteen months, I had a new scan of my back and found a fully relieved disc space, no apparent scar tissue but some calcification that I would probably have to contend with at some point.

I started physical therapy to learn how to work out with my new back. I was pain-free and able to run without a hitch on my way to a full recovery.

Heart Attack

In August 2008, my father called me as I was leaving a horse show with my dog in the truck and my horse in the trailer behind me to let me know that my mother was in the hospital. She had almost died of a heart attack that morning, he told me but she appeared to be stable now, and I should come and visit.

You think? So I took my horse home, unloaded the truck and the dog, and went to the hospital.

When I arrived on her hospital floor I heard yelling. It was mother. I followed the sound of her voice to her room where she was chewing out one of many nurses who had the misfortune to be on shift that night. Oh, she was feeling better all right, and she wanted to go home!

"All this is ridiculous!" she said. "Helena! If you ever loved me, you would take me home right now!"

Great, no treachery there. Thanks, Mom.

She was in the hospital for a week. Every night my father or I would bring something for the nurses to show our appreciation for their care and I would always greet them with a *hello* and *I'm sorry, thank you for not quitting* look.

It turns out that my mother had an ulcer from all the acetaminophen she was taking and had been bleeding most of the summer. When she became unable to respond to her name my father took her to the hospital. Once they admitted her she had a heart attack due to a hematocrit level of two. Most people die if their hematocrit goes to four or below. My father didn't know about the ulcer until my mother was in the hospital and stabilized. When he asked her why she hadn't said anything, she dismissed the question as though it was the most ridiculous thing a person could ask. Why on earth would she talk about it? It would heal eventually…

This was another major life-changing event for my mother but not in a way that I had hoped. She was very fearful of her new found weakness and even more fearful that she would fall down, get hurt, and have to go back to the hospital. She never wanted to go back to the hospital again. Ever!

Finally, I gained some insight into my mother's ongoing frustration with her life. She had a true mind-body disconnect. She viewed her body as a thing that weighed her down, bothering her with mundane functions and needs. At this point in her life, she had been struggling with high blood pressure for about twelve years. As a result, she suffered extreme headaches, decreased physical function, and listlessness from the medication. She was not a cooperative patient, rarely went to the doctor, and expected my dad to give her the medicines she needed.

Where was my husband during all of this? Estranged. I realized that my marriage was over. It had probably been over before it had begun and I hadn't been able to face it until now. Seeing my mother fight her own reality encouraged me to face my own. I had experienced too many betrayals and too many heartbreaks in my marriage, in my life. I decided that I would have rather lived the rest of my life alone than in this torture. It was time to file for divorce.

CHAPTER 6

Life's Lessons Should You Choose to See Them

My mother had started smoking cigarettes when she was twelve, this was taboo on many levels, but more on that later. So when she started to experience these health problems she was convinced it was a result of a lifetime of smoking. A rational fear. After the hospital visit in 2008 she stopped for a while but addictions are hard to quit cold turkey (or at all) and soon she was smoking again. My father agonized over her smoking and whether he should stop contributing to it. He was buying the cigarettes, since she rarely left the house.

When he stopped buying her cigarettes, Mom just had them delivered to her by the housekeeper (who wanted to stay on Mom's good side) and she rationed them. Dad soon gave up the fight until he noticed that in the summer of 2010 she was starting to shows signs of disorientation and confusion. The "spells" were temporary, but he wanted her to go to the doctor to get checked out. She refused. He stopped buying her cigarettes, and when she ran out, her mental condition worsened.

She became increasingly disoriented, needing someone at the house at all times to make sure that she didn't try to light a straw or something else passing as a cigarette on fire. Needless to say, this was a huge concern, again on many levels. As much as I wanted to lecture my father on the adverse effects of withdrawal and the importance of my mother going to the hospital, it was no use. My parents were stubborn and I could only do so much. My father finally took my mother to the hospital in October and she was admitted for two weeks.

Her kidneys were failing and her blood pressure was out of control. My mother was not a good candidate for dialysis, because even at the hospital she needed twenty-four-hour observation. She pulled her IVs out whenever no one was looking. Unfortunately, this was not the first time she had fought her treatment. In 2008, after being in the hospital for a few days, my mother felt well enough to pull out her IVs, insisting she was well enough to go home. The nurses had to restrain and sedate her in order to continue treatment. This hospitalization was no different. So my mother went from being despondent to irate with her circumstances. Remember, she had never wanted to be in a hospital again. She had been very clear with me the first time. So this was a betrayal.

The doctors tried to stabilize her kidneys and ran a multitude of tests to rule out any other contributing factors. She had a clean bill of health aside from her ongoing high blood pressure and her kidney's poor functioning. The doctors believed it was her unstabilized high blood pressure that led to her kidney failure and her regular intake of anti-inflammatories for her headaches. My mother's mental orientation improved once fully detoxed, as well as her kidney function, and she was released two weeks before Thanksgiving.

We had Thanksgiving at home, just the three of us. My father and I spoke daily about Mom's condition. He had the housekeeper come to the house when he was at work so Mom was not alone. I visited twice a week and I noted her decline. We had Christmas at the house, again just the three of us, and I talked about a new man I had met in person via an Internet dating site. It was a nice distraction from all the sadness and we mused about where this meeting could potentially lead.

I discussed with my father, separate from my mother, my concerns about her health and told him I thought she needed to go back to the hospital. Two days later, after seeing her general practitioner in his office, she went back into the hospital. Her kidney function had declined again, her mental orientation was worse than before, and, after a CAT scan, the doctors discovered significant brain atrophy...a result of the poor blood pressure.

My mother had been severely ill and a shadow of herself for eleven months now. She had been in and out of hospitals for six of those months. She was a terrible patient. Meaning she was uncooperative with at-home recommendations; she thought the hospital staff were a bunch of idiots and told them regularly she just wanted my father to fix this so she could go home to get better.

My father was the only doctor she trusted. He was a brilliant doctor, not only in her mind, but in the mind of almost everyone who had worked with him. He, too, was baffled as to why she couldn't get better. I, being the only child, having watched my family since early childhood knew, instinctually, that my mother would not live to see the year through. She had been dying of a broken heart for years, a diagnosis I knew and had tried to fix since I was small… Freud, eat your heart out.

My mother, who was known for her style and sophistication, was now reduced to a white T-shirt and adult diapers. She was easier to get along with now because she rarely spoke. But if you tried to help her with something and she didn't want you to help her…well, then you and everyone else within a block radius heard her opinion.

In the meantime, my father was feeling more lethargic. He was understandably tired and overwhelmed. He kept working to distract himself, seeking to affect someone in a positive way because the situation at home felt hopeless. And so it went until the end of May 2011.

CHAPTER 7

Trifecta

"Wow—it's like a trifecta for you."

—Stanley Rouhe, June 22, 2011

It was May 2011. My father was exhausted. He had not been feeling well since January and it was to no one's surprise given he was trying to maintain his business, be a part-time surgeon and a full-time caretaker/doctor to my mother. He has gone to various doctors to eliminate possibilities of a prostate cancer recurrence.

He was diagnosed in October 1996 with stage three prostate cancer. He elected to have surgery and radiation the following spring. After the surgery his doctor came out and told me had five years to live. I didn't tell my father this until the summer of 2014. It had been fourteen years since he was told he was in remission.

He had his hip replaced in 2008. The surgery went well and he was walking thirty minutes after he woke up. Full recovery took a few months and it only bothered him when he didn't exercise regularly.

So why was he not feeling well? A reoccurrence of prostate cancer was ruled out. He then wanted to see if his "new hip" was degrading. It wasn't, but his doctor found something else during an ultrasound of his chest cavity. On the last Friday in May 2011, he got the answer: stage four pancreatic cancer.

This was a death sentence. It is a very difficult cancer to find due to its insidious nature and lack of real symptoms. Once a person starts feeling bad it's still hard to diagnosis and then impossible to defeat. My hope is that this will change someday.

When he called to tell me, I was stunned. I couldn't believe it, and then again, given how drained he had been feeling it made sense. But when he said he only had six months or less to live, I shut down. He asked me to attend a special prayer session for him at his church that Sunday; aside from that I couldn't really tell you what I did that weekend. I was in shock. Frozen.

My question of when I should take a leave of absence from work to be home for my parents was answered.

I needed to take it then, for at least thirty days, with the option of sixty. Thankfully, my boss was very understanding and my team did a great job of stepping up to the plate. So I didn't worry about them even though I felt bad for leaving them so quickly. I took two days to get them organized and started my leave on June 1, the same day I placed my mother in home hospice.

Despite my asking my father not to tell my mother about his diagnosis until we had a plan of treatment, he chose to tell her the same night he told me. I couldn't begrudge him this; they were each other's best friends and compatriots; how could he not confide in her? My mother spent the rest of her time at home declining in both mental and physical capacity. She stared off into space most of the time and had long since given up caring about personal hygiene. It was terrible to see her in this state and my father's news only accomplished one thing. She was now determined to be the first one to die. Her rapid decline provided some comfort to my father. He knew that she would not allow anyone else to care for her, so if she went first then he could relax knowing I would not have to fight her to give her care.

Within the first few days of hospice we were visited by our case manager, doctor, and social worker. All were shocked to hear the circumstances: wife of forty-seven years in kidney failure and final stages of life refusing to eat or receive basic care due to husband's recent diagnosis of stage four pancreatic cancer; parents to one child here to help while on leave from work. They were all at a bit of a loss as to what to say to me. I was facing the death of both of my parents and very soon. The caregivers were kind and encouraged me to do whatever I needed to do to take care of myself during this difficult time.

Little did they know I was in crisis mode and would be for quite some time: "I got this."

My mother's remaining spirit wilted significantly every day. On day five of hospice, I finally broke down and cried while I held her hand and wished her peace and a smooth transition. The next day she perked up a little bit and it was good to make a connection with her. That night I decided to go home to get some rest. She passed away around 11:00 p.m. My father called me in tears and I rushed back to the house.

I had never seen a dead body before; the closest I'd ever come was at the National Museum of Tolerance in Washington, D.C. There was this amazing set of pictures of a man, who was a concentration camp prisoner, just released by American troops. The prisoner was standing in a doorway, leaning against the frame. In the next shot, everything is the same. His position has not changed, but he is dead. You could actually see the difference in the pictures between when he was alive and when he was dead. It was incredible. I stood there for a long while wondering how anyone could doubt that we have souls when we have such blatant proof.

As my boyfriend and I drove to my parents' house I was overwhelmed by emotions but I was eager to see my mother's body and my reaction to it: a weird statement, I know; perhaps I can explain as we go on.

When we arrived I hugged my father first and then went to her. I felt a strange sense of grief and relief. She was no longer suffering; her spirit was not there. *Thank you, Lord for taking my mother and relieving her of all this pain.* As we sat waiting for the nurse, who was called to pronounce my mother dead, I found myself becoming impatient. I wanted the body to be removed. This was not my mother. It was a shell. I didn't want that to be what I remembered; I didn't want to see it anymore. I finally got up and walked into the other room.

It was the middle of the night when the morticians came to collect my mother's body.

They came to the back door drifting into the light like spirits themselves. I was grateful I didn't scream when I saw their faces appear from out of the dark. They were kind, gracious with their condolences, and very respectful. When they left all I wanted to do was sleep but of course that didn't last for long. It was June 7; my mother had died within a week of being in hospice and within two weeks of learning of my father's diagnosis. She succeeded at being the first to die.

My father actually suggested that I wait to do a memorial for my mother and just do one for both of them when he passed! *Ridiculous*, was the first word out of my mouth, but I was soon checked when I noted the grief on his face. He was not prepared for how my mother's death would affect him. Later that same afternoon he said to me that he felt more connected to her now than he had in a long time. I told him I wasn't surprised; they'd had a strong bond and now there was nothing in the way of that bond. Mom was no longer fighting. She was at peace. I also knew that my father was not long for this world.

It's a strange thing to plan a memorial. When I was younger my mother and I used to joke about what I would do with her ashes: spread them among the roses (her favorite flowers) while sneezing in the process, place them in a mausoleum specially erected to her and visit them every day, toss them in the wind only to have them end up all over me. We could joke about these things because my parents and I had one definite thing in common and that is a belief in God. We believe, as human beings we have eternal souls. So the body is just a shell we are given to live out our earthly lives and then it's ashes to ashes, dust to dust. Thankfully, my parents and I discussed their wishes and mine in regard to their passing and how I wanted to remember them.

Ultimately, I didn't want to be limited by one space to visit them or ashes to be maintained or stored. Since I believe their souls are in heaven and my memories are with me, going to a certain location to show respect to them didn't make sense to me.

My mother's body was cremated. My father and I went to the mortuary the day after my mother passed away to make the arrangements. My father wrote a check in the family checkbook to cover the cost of this process, a checkbook I had once set up for my parents while managing their finances, a checkbook I would end up keeping myself.

My uncle Torgny, my mother's only sibling, came to visit for a week from Sweden. His original plan had been to visit with his sister before she passed, but now plans had changed and he was here for her memorial. I knew this visit would be hard on him. My mother was stubborn and she and her brother had their differences. For these reasons they had a rocky relationship. I'm sure he would have liked to connect with her before she passed, but, as I said, she hadn't been herself for years. The time for reconciliation and peace making had long since passed.

Torgny had always had a great affinity with my father and I was pleased they could spend time together. At the same time, I had a college friend visiting, who also came into town with the same original intentions as my uncle and was now helping me plan my mother's memorial. Once I convinced my father that Mom needed her own memorial, the rest was just a matter of organizing.

Another friend of mine, who is a gifted writer, was asked by my father to write my mother's memorial program—no pressure there, she kindly agreed. Well, actually, I think the conversation went more like this:

"J, dad wants to know if you would write the memorial program for Mom. What do you think?"

"He requested me specifically? What time do you want me to come over?"

I have included the program in the chapter about my mother.

My mother was most comfortable at home so this was where we held the memorial. I arranged for a gardener to give the grounds a good cleanup, ordered the flowers, food, and champagne. The later was actually a CostCo run with my father...our last outing. Odd. There is a Costco story. It will appear later.

My mother loved champagne so it was a must to have a toast during her memorial. My father went about these plans in a daze. Not only was it surreal that my mother was no longer here with us in body, but my father's health was now rapidly declining. He was now in his own final stretch.

The morning of my mother's memorial, just five days after she passed, he talked to me about starting him on home hospice. He was having increased pain and difficulty sleeping and eating.

He said, "Don't worry about it today. If something happens, there will be a lot of doctors here so they can help."

All I wanted to say was WHAT THE !@#$, but instead I swallowed hard and said, "OK, we can call home hospice tomorrow. Is that all right?"

"Yes," he said, "I can wait."

My mother's memorial ended up being the first time in about twenty years that people were invited to my parents' house. (I will explain the reasons behind this later). Naturally, curiosity took over as they wandered the house: a museum to my mother and our family. Everyone who came to the memorial came to pay their respects to my mother but also to see my father. All of my cousins on my dad's side attended, and since they were spread out across the country, this was a real feat. This was endearing and frustrating to me. We were there to acknowledge my mother, not to say goodbye to my father! He was still alive, but, in fact, his cancer was on a fast track and it proved to be the exact right thing to do. Because, in fact, for most people in attendance, it was their time to say goodbye to him as well. Upon reflection (actually this was my boyfriend, Randy's, statement to me while I was frustrated, but I'm now adopting it because I know he was right), what an amazing gift it was to have everyone you love and care for in one place so that you can visit with them and say goodbye before you leave this world. It meant a great deal to my father to have this experience, and I decided that from then on, this house would be open to visitors for my father, regardless of how long he had to live.

WHITE DRESS

I spoke at my mother's memorial. I knew I would regret it if I didn't say something. I wore a white form-fitting dress that my mother had given me fifteen years before and told the following story:

My mother liked giving gifts. So when she offered me a gift, with no particular reason, I wasn't surprised. However, at this point, it was rare for her to buy me clothes. We had very different tastes and she had, for the most part, given up on dressing me. But she saw this dress at Nordstrom and knew it would look great on me.

The conversation we had when she presented it to me went something like this: "Thank you, Mom; I really appreciate you buying me something, but I'm not really sure where I would wear it." (The dress is form-fitting...no room for error in form-fitting, floor-length, and made of a Lycra–cotton blend.) Her response was, "What do you mean? It's so versatile." (She wasn't kidding.)

"You could wear it as a cover-up to the beach, you could wear it on a casual night out with friends, or even a BBQ."

"Really, Mom, like any of those options are realistic for me. I could see *you* wearing this to one of those events but not me. But I do appreciate the gesture and I'm sure I'll think of something."

Over the years it sat in my closet. I looked at it often and considered it for many occasions but it just never seemed quite right. Then it just became a source of amusement for me and a great example of how different my mother and I were from each other. And now I have the perfect occasion…

The story got great laughs and many relieved faces, because who wears a white, form-fitting floor-length dress to their mother's funeral and claims they are mourning? My mother loved white so it really was the perfect thing to wear. She was right.

SAYING GOODBYE

The next day we started my father in hospice, and two days later we had another hospital bed delivered in the room my mother had previously inhabited. This was no déjà vu; this was surreal. I spent the week hosting our family and friends and getting my parents' financial affairs in order. Unfortunately, despite my asking and pleading for the better part of twenty years to please get this done, it had not gotten done. There was a lot of work to do and time was running out. So I had to research the best way to proceed and then make the arrangements. My father said he would hold on until the documents were complete and everything was in order for me to take over without question.

When my friend Adrienne was getting ready to leave for the airport, she went in to say goodbye to my father and he said, "Well, this is goodbye until I see you on the other side." He said, "Thank you for coming, for being such a great friend to my daughter. Thank you for being here with us through this difficult time. Anne-Louise always liked you and she was glad that you and Helena were friends. Take care of each other, take care of your family, and take care of yourself."

I can still picture the whole scene. It was too much for me to watch, but as I looked down at the ground I heard his words. He was saying goodbye to both of us. It was heartbreaking.

A few days later, my uncle Torgny took his turn to say goodbye. They shared a long knowing look and then my uncle said, "Well, this is goodbye for now," and my father said, "This is goodbye for now." They stood in a long embrace shedding tears for their years together and the loss of their physical connection. The next time they meet it would be better but it would be different. It is sad to let go of the familiar. This time I was able to watch through tear-filled eyes but I refused to let this goodbye apply to me. I knew the truth; it was another goodbye from my father to his daughter through my uncle.

I enjoyed hosting people at the house. It was a unique time when we could all visit, share stories, walk down memory lane with my father, and bond. I was grateful for my therapy background. I found the words to say to people I barely knew who were faced with my father's impending death. I would slip in and out of professional mode and it gave me focus in this unbearable time. I created a rotation for family to spend the night and care for my dad when I needed to run errands or just needed a break. My father was glad for the time he spent with his siblings and extended family. He had regular visitors who would come over for dinner and just hang out. It was a magical time.

However, his discomfort was increasing with each day. His last meal ended up being at my mother's memorial. He couldn't keep food down now. His liver had so grossly enlarged that it made it difficult for him to breathe, and he had to shift around a lot to find relief.

On June 22, my old border collie, one of two dogs my parents kept at the house, died of natural causes. She was sixteen and had slowed down considerably in the previous two months. It was not a surprise, and yet I was sad when I found her in the backyard. However, I was glad I found her rather than any of my other family members, who had enough to deal with given the circumstances. Yes, I was definitely in crisis mode.

I debated whether I should tell my father, but in the end I knew he would want to know where she was so I walked back up to the house. I found my father sitting up in his hospital bed talking to his sister, his business partner, his partner's wife and office manager.

I said, "Well, I have news. Ireland [her name] died."

My aunt Suzanne said, "What! Are you serious?"

I said, "Yeah, it's not a surprise really, but it is sad and I'm glad I'm the one who found her."

Everyone was silent and then my father, true to form, said, "Wow, it's like a trifecta for you."

"Really, Dad, jeez, well, I'm not planning on digging a hole for you anytime soon," I said as I shook my head and went back outside to find a shovel.

HERE'S A SHOVEL. NOW GO DIG A HOLE.

Now, you have my permission to tap into your macabre sense of humor here, because if you can't laugh at this next part… Well, sometimes humor just makes things easier to hear.

Just as I was walking out of the house, Randy walked up from another part of the house. I said, "Hey, I need to talk to you outside, "

"OK," he said, apprehensively…with reason at this point.

"OK, what's up?"

"Ireland died."

"Are you serious?" (Really, people! Oh, no, I'm just kidding. I just wanted to see your reaction…I thought it would be funny. Umm, no, just kidding!)

"Oh. I'm so sorry," he said and gave me a hug."

Here's the good part: I said, "So I need you to dig a hole in the chicken coop."

"What? Let's just call animal control."

"No, it's too late and I want to bury her myself." Meaning, *I need you to dig the hole and I will help cover her body.* (I went to get a shovel and handed it to him.) "So start digging a hole and I'll be down there in a minute to help."

"But I've never done this before; I don't know how big of a hole to dig."
He was looking for a way out.

My response? "Well, I don't want to see her anymore, so dig it that big.
You will pass her on the way down the hill, so that will give you an idea. Now,
go on. I'll be down there soon."

At this point, I walked back into the house to tell everyone my plan,
gather the necessary items to complete the job, and head to the chicken coop,
where I found my boyfriend of six months digging a hole. It was sweltering
hot outside and humid, totally miserable, but what a trooper! I tried to help,
which is not saying much, since I think I added more dirt than I dug out.
Once we thought we were ready, we collected Ireland's body and took her to
her final resting place. Now, to say that I was emotionally overwhelmed and
strung out at this point is an understatement. We placed her in the grave and
I panicked for just a second and looked at Randy and said, "Do you think she
is really dead?" (She was clearly dead.)

"Yes, honey, I'm sorry." (What a trooper.)

I quickly responded, "Ireland, you were a good dog!!" and we buried her.
God bless crisis mode.

I can't believe I'm doing this runs through my mind. This was my father's
job when I was a kid. I couldn't believe she had died. I was glad she didn't suffer long, and she must have known that her job of watching out for my parents
was done. If I only knew.

The next day was my worst nightmare.

The lawyer sent over two lovely women to get the final paperwork signed
so everything in my parents' estate was in a trust. My father stated he had
wanted this done a week earlier. Now that everything was organized this was
the last step. All he needed to do was sign the papers.

He was getting weaker by the day and something so simple turned out
to be almost too much. It was my last straw. So halfway through the process,
when he said, "Can we finish this tomorrow? I'm tired," I snapped. In front of
two of my aunts, an uncle, and these two lovely ladies I screamed at my father,

on his deathbed. My worst nightmare. "There is no more time! The thing I have being asking from you and trying to avoid for the past twenty years has come to pass. You have to sign the papers TODAY!" I thought to myself, *He has to sign these papers and this is his will but he is tired and just wants to be done.* I couldn't believe this was happening. I looked and felt like a money-grubbing schemer and I just wanted to throw up, pull my hair out, and join Ireland in the chicken coop. After yelling the gist of this to my father with the audience to witness, I stormed out of the house in hysterics.

I called Randy and described the scene, saying I was convinced all these people viewed me as a terrible person and I needed him. He hopped on his motorcycle and came to my rescue. (I don't want to think about how many laws he broke.) In the meantime, another girlfriend just happened to call and I ranted and cried to her. Then my poor uncle came and found me: "Helena, they need you to finish the papers; everything is signed."

"Everyone thinks I'm a terrible person. I'm so embarrassed."

He said, "Don't be ridiculous" and led me back to the house. The gracious ladies finished the papers with me and I apologized multiple times. They were kind and understanding. At this point Randy came blazing in, ready for a fight, to defend me against these judgmental jerks! I interceded as soon as he got there and explained the truth of things. At this point, we were both exhausted.

My father was sad but understanding of the situation. I apologized for my behavior and he waved me off. He understood and felt bad it had come to this; we acknowledged our love for each other and left it at that. The next day he was noticeably relaxed and quiet. He was dying, and the home hospice nurse said it would be soon. That night I stayed next to my father and held his hand.

Peaceful Music

When my mother was in hospice I would leave the TV on the blues/jazz station to play her favorite music. She seemed to relax when it was on. It also helped people who were visiting her feel more at ease.

When my father was in hospice, I asked him what music he wanted. He said, "Speed Station." For him the sound of motors revving, passing one another at crazy speeds and the *vroom-vroom* of a Grand Prix brought a smile to his face. To this day, I can't hear Grand Prix racing without thinking of him.

The last ten days of my father's life became a comforting routine of close family and friends coming by to visit. My father's brothers and sister spent the night in rotations and spent the evenings visiting with one another in my father's room. It was a large room on the first floor next to the kitchen so it was easy to host these gatherings. My father was greatly comforted by these visits and it was also a comfort to all of us to support one another through this time of transition. We were all still accepting my mother's death and trying to wrap our heads around my father's daily decline. It was a special time for us all, a bonding time that brought us closer to one another in a way that none of us could have predicted.

It was my night to stay with my father, the night he passed. Normally, the people staying the night stayed in the bedroom directly above his room so that he could have some alone time (his request). But on this night I felt like I needed to stay with him. At first, I tried to sleep on the couch behind his bed but it wasn't comfortable and I didn't feel right. Nothing felt right. I was restless and checked on him every few minutes. I finally just moved a chair right next to his bed and held his hand. This was very out of character for our family. We did not hug or hold hands. But all previous family pretense was out the window. I needed to touch him, to feel what was going on in his body.

At around three in the morning, he began really struggling to breathe. Breathing had become increasingly difficult with each passing day and he would have to adjust regularly to find a comfortable spot. This time was different. He couldn't get comfortable. I said, "Dad, how can I help?" Softly, with his eyes closed, he said, "This is it." Then, shortly thereafter, he became really impatient and he said to his body, "Come on, now, let go!" It was quiet, almost a mumble, but I sat there in shock as I processed what I knew I had heard.

I continued to hold his hand as he and his body had their last fight. I tried to keep him comfortable with the medication pump, but it could only do so much. I cried and moaned as my dad let go of his mortal coil. This was the most painful thing I have ever had to witness. I was so upset and yet I was equally grateful that I could be there to hold his hand. The process felt like it took forever, and when he finally let go I passed out from grief and exhaustion. I woke up at five thirty in the morning to discover that my father was dead. He was no longer in his body and his body looked very similar to mother's body just a few weeks before. And yet for just the briefest moment, as with my dog just a few days before, I questioned, *Is he really gone; did he really die?* It was obvious what had happened but still difficult to comprehend, even though I was there and had witnessed the whole thing.

My father passed away on June 25, 2011. Just eighteen days after my mother.

I went through the motions of calling the nurse, who called the mortician and I met again the same two morticians, who couldn't believe we were doing this again so soon. They were so young; how could this be? I texted one of my aunts, who let our immediate family know. The golf crew, my dad's closest friends, were on the course and came up to pay their respects. My aunt came to the house to sit with me. They were all gracious and kind to me while mourning the loss of their beloved family member and friend. Then, when all was said and done, they left me (as I requested) in the big old house alone with my thoughts. It was the way I needed it to be.

All too soon, I was planning my father's memorial. My same girlfriend did the program, another incredible life sketch, complete with pictures we picked out together. I was numb, expertly going through the motions, relieved that neither of my parents were burdened any longer with pain or discomfort. Grateful for my faith, I prayed for strength and determination. I wanted the speech for my father's memorial to be a reflection of him and acknowledgment of both of my parents.

My speech for my father's memorial on July 7, 2011:

A month ago, to the day, I lost my mother. Now today we are here to celebrate the memories of a great man, who affected and forever influenced us all, my father.

My parents passed away within three weeks of each other from separate medical illness and yet, despite the speed with which this has all happened, I'm not surprised.

Why, you ask? Well, my parents would say, good question. Not because of the circumstances but because in our house it was a sign of intelligence to ask why and to seek out a complete and sensible answer. Both of my parents were eternal students.

They loved to learn.

Every day was an opportunity to improve your knowledge and prepare for the night's discussion.

Topics to be covered ranged from current political events, the state of the government and its progress or downfall, the current state of a particular culture and how they have evolved from their historical predecessors... all of these topics where riddled with references to literature read recently or during their education. In other words, my parents were ridiculously intelligent and fed their brains daily. It was no mistake my father was a brain mechanic.

I laughed when I had a professor once announce in class that the best answer to the question "Why?" was "Because." I thought *what an amateur*; my mother would eat you for lunch and my father would say you had it coming.

You see, I can't talk about one of my parents without discussing the other. They were a pair, a matched set. And that is why I will try to explain why we are gathered here today.

My mother would tell you she and my father were babies when they met, fell in love and got married, since all of this happened prior to their twenty-first birthdays.

I would tend to agree. My mother said my father was the most gorgeous man she had ever met. She was infamous for instant impressions, and when it came to my father it was adoration at first sight!

My father would tell you that my mother was instantly attractive to him not just because of her beauty but because she carried herself with such confidence and intelligence. She was a force to be reckoned with, a delightful challenge.

This was their existence: to challenge and engage one another in interesting debates and unique adventures. My job was to keep up with these two intellectual powerhouses as well as to create my own path.

I used humor to keep our little merry band of three entertained while we flew down the autobahn of life.

I loved to make my father laugh because his laugh was contagious and my mother was sure to follow.

My father's laugh always started the same way. He got a glimmer in his eyes, followed by a smirk on his lips, a giggle in his belly, and finally a tear down his cheek.

I will miss his laugh.

My father's favorite comedian was Steve Martin.

As I was preparing what to say tonight I kept thinking of the song from *The Sound of Music*: "How do you solve a problem like Maria?" Except I would call it "What do you say about a man like Stanley" and have it sung by Steve Martin, but, alas, that wasn't possible, so you'll just have to imagine it.

Why are we here tonight?

My mother has been seriously ill since last October and my father was the only one she would allow to treat her because he was the only one, she felt, who understood her. This was difficult for both of them.

But it was expected since it was how they led their lives.

My father suspected he had something wrong with him a few months ago, but pancreatic cancer is hard to diagnosis. So when it was diagnosed, it was too late to treat.

That was all my mother needed to hear. Whatever fight she had in her was gone; my father was dying and she decided she was going first. She passed within two weeks of knowing my father's diagnosis.

Within twenty-four hours of her passing my father turned to me and said, "I feel more connected to your mother now than I have in years."

My response was, "She is no longer battling her physical self. Now you have a pure connection," and I knew at that moment my father was not long for this world. The next day he said he would stick around long enough to get his affairs in order. So I hustled to make that happen and opened the house to visitors so they could say their goodbyes. And within twenty-four hours of completing his affairs, my father joined my mother in heaven.

We are here tonight because my parents are soul mates, and although they died of different medical causes, they couldn't live without each other. So, take comfort in this: they are with our Heavenly Father, they are together, and they are at peace. Thank you for coming to celebrate a great man and his soul mate. God bless!

I took about a week to be on my own. I needed time to decompress, absorb, accept. I drove to Park City, Utah, a frequent family vacation spot. I found the time away from everything very healing. I began to gain some insight into our family dynamic as I wandered around; some of this I have already shared. It was a good trip and when I returned home, I had about a week to prepare for the next trip.

I decided after my mother passed away I was going to go to Sweden to have a memorial there for my family who had been unable to attend the memorial at my parents' house. Now it would be a double memorial and even more important to me to be around all of my family.

On July 31, 2011, we had a joint memorial for my parents at my youngest cousin's house in Falkenberg, Sweden. It was a small group of us, which turned out to be really nice. We were all able to freely share stories about both my parents and relate the shock of how quickly everything happened. I also made a point of spending time with close family friends on this trip, allowing me to connect with good memories of my parents and times we were all together. They had known both of my parents since college and my mother since she was in grade school. We were able to discuss the last few years from a different perspective. I realize now it was this time that inspired me to write down my experiences. These memories were too amazing and their stories too special to be forgotten.

There is much more to tell about this time in my life, but I will segue here to my parents so that you can get a sample of their story, how fantastic they were, and what drew them together.

CHAPTER 8

The Mystery that Was Anne-Louise Brigitta Sonestam Rouhe

My mother was born in Stockholm, Sweden, in 1943—right after the war, as she would say. She was her father's daughter: precocious, curious and willful. Well, she got that from both sides, it turns out. She started reading books at a very early age and adored discussing them with her father. Much to her dismay, her brother was born when she was five. She was no longer the star of the show and actually spent some time in France with some of her mother's relatives to allow her mother time to adjust. My mother made the best of it and turned the time in France into an adventure and the people into stars to be wondered at.

My grandfather was a Seventh Day Adventist (SDA) pastor. At the time, the typical Swede was Lutheran, so to be SDA was unusual, let alone a pastor. My grandfather was one of three pastors named Svenson (all brothers) in the same area of southwest Sweden, so he changed his name to Sonestam (stone stem or foundation), a name he created to eliminate confusion. The expectation for pastors and their families was to provide an example to the community, and you did not draw attention to yourself. This soon became a problem for my mother, who was born to be opinionated, willful, and independent. For example, when my uncle was three, my mother (eight) decided to cut off his eyelashes because she read in a fashion magazine it would make them grow back longer and fuller. My grandmother was understandably appalled and my mother was punished. But in true Anne-Louise fashion, she had the last laugh because my uncle has great eyelashes.

In turn, my uncle Torgny has a great story about my mother from when they were kids. He told this story at my mother's memorial. It was the first time I had heard it. Apparently, when my uncle was four or five he would chase my mother around the house. Inevitably, they would end up upstairs, where she would barricade herself into her room. Her door would open a few inches, just enough to see in and then it wouldn't budge, sending him into a frenzy that would soon tire him out, leaving her alone to her thoughts. The mystery of how my mother managed the "door trick" exasperated my uncle for years. When my mother went away to boarding school at the age of twelve, he snuck into her room and discovered her secret. She would prop a big book between the radiator and the door so the door would open but only a little bit. *Brilliant*, he thought.

My mother made this or other striking impressions wherever she went. She was curious and adventurous and carried herself with such poise that people often mistook her for someone really important: royalty or the child of a tycoon. Instead, she was a pastor's daughter who was supposed to just blend in: be a good example to other children her age. Although her lasting impressions did not go over with her parents, her father couldn't help but enjoy her zest for life. Her mother, my grandmother, was not nearly as amused and this established a lifelong history of angst between the two.

As I mentioned, my mother went to boarding school(s). I say "schools" because she went to several. The Seventh Day Adventist school system was rather diverse in its locations throughout Europe. So my mother went to a different one each year to learn different languages. She had a gift for language and could passably speak eight different ones, some more proficiently than others.

My mother's first real scandal occurred during her first year of boarding school, Eykbyholm. She was friendly with a boy her age (twelve) and they were caught walking together alone. The headmaster was appalled by this behavior. Notice a theme here.

The two were separated and the families were called. My grandfather was a proud man and refused to have his daughter associated with such scandalous behavior. Both children were pulled out of the school. My uncle didn't know what happened to the boy. I found out later he was transferred to another school. She went to school in town, forty-five minutes from where her parents live. She took the train in and out every day. School was six days a week.

While she was attending the city school she became involved in local theater. Scandal rocked the family again when my mother starred in a play, got rave reviews in the local paper, and my grandmother's friends called to tell her about it. My grandparents were mortified that my mother would draw such attention to herself and therefore the family. She was pulled out of the play.

She also decided to dye her brunette hair jet black. My grandmother sent her back to the hairstylist immediately to return it to her natural color. These fights and many more contributed to my mother wanting to attend school far away from home.

EYKBYHOLM

As a side note, in 2013 I went back to Sweden to spend time with family. I asked Barbro, my mother's oldest and dearest friend, if we could visit Eykbyholm since I had heard so many stories set there. She delighted in the idea and off we went to return to childhood memories. We toured the main building and walked the grounds while she recounted stories of my mother. We met a man who approached us by saying to Barbro, "I recognize that face." She introduced herself and me, adding that I am Anne-Louise Sonestam's daughter.

"Anne-Louise Sonestam," he said in near rapturous terms. "Anne-Louise Sonestam, she was so, so…" Barbro added, "Striking?"

"Yes!" he said. "So striking!"

He threw in something about my being striking too since I was her daughter but it felt like a bit of an afterthought to account for his distracted thoughts. Then he proceeded to tell us about the last time he had seen my mother, in 1958. "She was with this boy…" He and Barbro had a discussion about who it was. Once they agreed, he continues to recount how lovely she was, and how was she now? He was so enamored of his memory Barbro and I both felt we were just bystanders at this point and simultaneously felt he was hoping my mother might be available to say hello to an old friend. Once I realized he wanted an answer to the question of how was my mother was today I had to tell him she had passed away. He paused, sad to hear the news, but then was back in his daydream of a better, sweeter time.

In 1960, she went to Neubold, a SDA college in England, and met my father who was back to finish his first year in college after a previously appreciated stay. This will be discussed in the following chapter. My mother went to school with her lifelong friend, Barbro. I have heard several stories from different people about my mother and Barbro at Neubold: of how these two would saunter across the quad and leave a lasting impression wherever they went. They were the Swedish beauties and intelligent to boot! My father was quite smitten but shy. So within the first week of classes my mother had determined that he was to be hers and the "German girl" who had her sights on him at the Friday night movie better clear off! She did and he was hers. They were together ever since. That was fifty years for those of you who are counting.

After a year at Neubold, my father was off to Southern Missionary College (SMC) outside Nashville, Tennessee. At the time, he was a religious studies major and wanted to continue at SMC, where the religious studies department was stronger. My mother went to Cologne, a SDA college in France, for the first semester and then on to SMC the second semester. To her dying day, my mother, would have told you she came to the United States to experience America. She was a history major and had always loved the history of the United States, its beginnings, its tragedies, and its successes. What better excuse to see it in action than during school? My father had a great telegram from my mother letting him know she had arrived in New York. It simply said, "The Statue of Liberty green! Disappointed. Chattanooga 13:40."

He was in love, and how could you not be with someone so wide-eyed about the world, so impressionable and mysterious? Two months after her arrival she was nominated as the princess of the courtesy court. It turns out everyone at SMC was smitten; she was a big hit.

Despite, my mother not coming to the United States to follow my father, she did follow him again to Northern California, where they spent the last two years of college at Pacific Union College (PUC), in St. Helena. Perhaps she went to sample the wine, since it is in the heart of wine country, and she was a rebel. SDAs do not drink alcohol, so we will blame the French side of the family for this behavior. At this point my father changed his major to biology/pre-med and was solidly on his course to follow in his father's footsteps. (More on that later.) My mother was a challenge to all the history professors and created quite an interesting reputation as an excellent debater.

My parents got married at the age of twenty, just shy of their twenty-first birthdays, but still. The wedding occurred in August 1964 between their junior and senior years of college. They chose to get married in Sweden, at Hultfaors, a SDA sanitarium and the church site where my grandfather was the minister and my grandmother was the administrator. My father's parents, sister, and one brother went to the wedding and were a part of the wedding party. My mother had her brother and closest, dearest friends stand by her. She designed the bridesmaids dresses, of course, and had them sewn to fit each bridesmaid. Exquisite taste. They honeymooned in Europe and then came back to the states, to PUC, to finish their degrees.

The early years of their marriage were spent in Loma Linda, California, where my father went to medical school. He graduated in 1969 and started his neurosurgery residency. My mother worked as an assistant to an interior designer in the area and considered it a career but ultimately didn't feel it was enough of a challenge. She also worked in a dress shop, where she helped customers spend lots of money. On her last day of an amicable parting, she owed the store money because she had bought so many things with her employee discount.

While working for an interior designer she scoped out many old homes in the area. She loved the Spanish villas or Victorians as long as they had an interesting story. So when she found the house in Queen Terrace from 1933, built with New Orleans flare for the builder's soon-to-be wife, it was a perfect fit. I was six months old when we moved into the house that became our family home of forty years.

My mother enjoyed family life. She enjoyed buying nice dresses and playing dolls with me as a toddler. This was her only time to influence my dressing because when I got older her dressing me was not going to happen. My mother became restless and needed a challenge so she decided to become a lawyer, a perfect fit for her interests in history, political science, and debate.

She attended a local school and again made lasting impressions. I recently ran into one of her professors, who said he really enjoyed her sitting in the front row because she was so striking. It was not surprising to hear but slightly odd at the same time since it came somewhat unsolicited. Her graduation photo shows her beaming from ear to ear. She was very happy. She promptly ordered herself calling cards: white with an embossed border and her name in simple classic black ink—Anne-Louise Sonestam Rouhe JD. She decided to order some for both herself and my dad, just in case: Dr. and Mrs. Stanley Allen Rouhe. They ended up as luggage tags.

My mother procured an office in an early 1900s building in downtown Riverside, ten minutes from our house. I was taking ballet classes at the time, much to the chagrin of myself and everyone else in the class. I would walk just one block away to my mother's office after practice. The office was decorated with vintage furniture beautifully crafted. It was a corner office with great arched windows. Her office business cards were equally beautiful and mimicked the look of the windows as they opened to reveal her information. She had the office for about two years. My father said that my mother loved the idea of practicing law but the practicalities of running a business—billing and keeping files—was annoying. Since our house was large and vintage like the furniture in the office it fit in quite well when she brought it home.

I have since discovered she never passed the bar exam despite trying many times. She used to tell me she was never a "good test taker" but I never knew about her bar exam results. The last time she took the exam was in 1981 and I believe this is why she was so willing to distract herself with my horse show career, which took off around the same time. This was also the same year that *Raiders of the Lost Ark* came out in movie theaters. My mother and I saw it nine times that summer.

I don't think disappointed even begins to cover her feelings around this time. Of course, not knowing any of this, I thought her feelings were about me. Kids have a tendency to take on their parents' stuff.

So now she had found herself to be my equine patron. This was a surprising turn of events for the whole family really. My mother liked the idea of my riding horses since it was elegant and the riding habit was classic. The day-to-day routine was not so glamorous, but to her credit she would pick me up from school and out we went to the barn about thirty minutes away. I would clean my pony, ride, get her bran mash together, and put her back in her stall. I loved it and my mother did enjoy watching me have such a good time.

She found the people who patronize the equestrian world were not really glamorous either. Oftentimes, people would spend money on their horses rather than on clothes, houses, education. So they were well meaning but not very interesting to her. She read a lot of books while at the ranch with me. About a year after I got my first pony, I graduated to a quarter horse, a fancy black show horse, to be specific, and my show career had begun. This kicked my horse schedule into overdrive. I trained for about two hours every day and did homework in the car going to and from the barn. My mother was not left with a lot of time to herself except for when I was in school or on the weekends, when my dad would take me to the barn.

After another year my mother was convinced by my horse trainer that I needed my horse to ride in the Western classes and a new horse to ride in the English classes. So we got a new addition. Also it could be her horse if she wanted to learn how to ride. That didn't happen but she did get riding pants, boots, and cute tops just in case she changed her mind. After two years, I got another Western horse. I was doing really well on the regional circuit and had been state champion in many categories. It was time to keep moving on, trying for bigger and better. With each horse came more time committed to the barn. My mother was a trooper and never complained—at least not to me.

We switched trainers, and I got another horse to replace the first English horse. The first two were now being bred, so we could either sell the foals or train them as future show horses. Our stable was growing and my parents decided to invest in a ranch in Temecula. The commute to the barn would be fifteen minutes longer each way but it would be ours and my mother could run it. Well, running a ranch is not as easy as she had thought. She did well for the most part, until someone questioned her authority and then things got heated.

With the new ranch came more horses, breedings, and show conquests. By the time I received the ranch to disperse for college money, we had fifteen horses. I kept one, which I had for a total of nineteen years before he died from leukemia at the age of twenty-two.

After my parents decided to sell the ranch, they wanted a new investment. They found another unique property in Lake Arrowhead called Little Bear Lodge (LBL). It was originally owned by the Temple family, of Shirley Temple fame. It was on one of the largest plots of land right on the lake, located straight across from the village. The original house was built in 1919 and all additions were finished by 1927. It was huge and a lot of work. But my mother absolutely loved it.

The area reminded my mother of Sweden but was nicer since the weather was more temperate and she was more at home now in the United States. Sweden had changed too much for her taste and she complained about it often. Her visits to Sweden had become sparse with her plate being so full from law school, my riding career, and working in my father's office. Working together turned out to be quite an adventure for my parents. I believe LBL kept them from getting a divorce.

It was the mid-1990s and medical insurance reimbursement had significantly changed. My father was concerned about his office and my mother decided to intervene. She brought in new staff, finding an office manager who stayed with my father in his business ventures until he died. She was a great find.

While LBL was being renovated, I lived in the house. This was during the time when I was teaching, so I taught at the local high school. In the summer of 1995, my family went to Sweden to celebrate my grandfather's eighty-fifth birthday. Birthdays every fifth or tenth year are a big deal in Sweden and often treated as a three-day affair, including hosting immediate family at your house for dinner, a big luncheon the following day, and the third day hosting friends and family for coffee and cookies. The visitors are expected to bring flowers. I have great pictures of my grandfather surrounded by flowers. My grandfather was an intense man and a bit of a poet. He delivered many speeches and seemed especially serious on this visit. He gave out a collection of poems and sermons to both my mother and my uncle at his birthday dinner.

A month after we got back from that trip, we found out my grandfather had pancreatic cancer. My mother flew back to Sweden within a week of hearing the news. She asked me to help out at my dad's office until she returned. She was there a month. Her father passed away. My mother refused to have my father or me come to Sweden for the funeral. She wanted to know everything was squared away at home. So we respected her wishes and stayed home. My family in Sweden later informed me of her state: my mother was beside herself, mentally absent or completely distraught the whole time, totally understandable given the circumstances but concerning since she was traveling alone.

When my mother returned home, she could not sleep in her own bed. She related the bed to her father's deathbed. She stayed on the couch with the TV on for comfort and distraction. She slept when she passed out from exhaustion. She asked me to take over the office and the finances. I worked this into my schedule while I was starting my PhD program at University of California, Riverside (UCR). My mother moved into LBL full time and shortly thereafter I moved back to my parents' house in Riverside. My mother made it very clear there was not enough room for the two of us.

Living in my parents' house was supposed to be temporary. My parents were mainly in Lake Arrowhead, the Riverside house needed someone to watch over it, and my dad wanted me to stick around. I did.

My mother was overwhelmed by her father's passing and she withdrew from everyone. She was short-tempered and obviously depressed, but she refused to seek treatment or get any kind of help. Her blood pressure became erratic, and her resulting headaches were unbearable. She was miserable.

My father was not feeling well and discovered a few months later that he had prostate cancer. This really devastated my mother. So things just went from bad to worse. I was determined to be helpful, so I took on my new role of bookkeeper with special zeal. I would bring in boxes of papers from the family account to go through papers and create a system. He predicted it would take five to six years to get things in order and out of debt. It took eight.

My father opted for radical surgery, and in post op his surgeon came to my mother and me in the waiting room to let us know how things had gone. The surgery went well; all the cancer had been removed, but there were no guarantees. My father's doctor took me aside and said that the cancer had spread farther than initially thought. There were places that may have been compromised that could not be removed in surgery. He recommended radiation and gave my father five years to live...at the most. I decided not to tell my mother.

The surgery was hard on my father, the radiation no easier. But he went back to work as soon as he was able, and life just went on. My mother's condition did not really improve, either. My father lived between two houses because of his work schedule and wanting a break from my mother's depression.

Two years later, my father decided he wanted his youngest brother, Lyndon, who had Down syndrome, to come live with us. On some level my father knew his time was short. He wanted to spend more time with Lyndon regardless of the consequences to our family. I didn't mind. I understood his motivations.

This was difficult for my mother, but it did break up her routine to some degree. I think he helped her. Lyndon ended up being an instrumental change in both my parents' lives. I will elaborate more on my father's changes later. My mother decided to host a few gatherings at the house. She decided to make the best of the circumstances, and for a few years she had a quiet but good routine.

Lyndon lived with my parents for about two years before it became too difficult for him and them. He needed more care than they could provide.

I met my husband (now ex) while all of this was going on; we had been dating for a couple of years. My mother's increased frustration with my relationship placed a significant strain on my relationship with her. We argued about everything. I felt she was very negative about any of my opinions. She was not happy with my decision to leave my first graduate program and even less thrilled with me becoming a therapist. My mother's opinion of therapists or psychology in general was that they were a waste of time. She believed that people don't change.

My parents took several trips to Europe during this time period, the early 2000s, to visit friends and family or have an adventure. The only problem with the adventure part was that my mother had become significantly less adventurous. She preferred spending her time in nice hotels versus going on a lot of day trips. This placed a strain on my parents' relationship. They were both frustrated with each other.

When my father retired in the summer of 2003, my mother was hoping they could start over somewhere else. Perhaps invest in a new house, maybe in Europe. Instead my father started one of many unsuccessful business ventures;

thankfully, for his sake, the last one was successful. In the meantime, between the strain of unsuccessful business ventures, one after another, and my disastrous relationship and impending marriage, my mother was very unhappy with our little family.

I can understand why. I wish I could have listened to her concerns. But my ex was so dismissive of my mother's tirades at this point, and I listened to him instead of her underlying concerns, which were valid. My father also struggled not to react to my mother's venom. It was serious stuff, and we bonded through our survival.

In order for my parents to be debt free in anticipation of my father's retirement, they needed to sell a house. My father chose to sell the Lake Arrowhead property. I knew this would break my mother's heart, but it was also the best time to sell. There was a real problem with bark beetles plaguing the trees of the area. My father paid outrageous water bills to keep the trees healthy. Trees that were not properly watered could not defend themselves and died. My mother did not help my father pack, and she refused to have me help since it was my fault the house was being sold. So my father and the movers packed everything.

When the house sold, many of the trees succumbed to the bark beetles. A month later the entire area was plagued with major fires and thousands of trees died from the bark beetles. My mother was glad they had sold the house, but the sale was bittersweet. Most of the boxes ended up at the Riverside house in the large garage, the basement, and workshop. The furniture, for the most part, ended up at a warehouse my uncles shared. The boxes were never opened. My mother was now back in Riverside, under the same roof as my father full time, and still not sleeping in a bed. She was depressed again and refused to go out or have people over to visit.

She did rally when my back went out in the beginning of 2005. Again, this broke up her routine and she started to go out on occasion and visit with friends. Then in 2008, she got a stomach ulcer from the overuse of anti-inflammatories and acetaminophen to manage terrible headaches, the result of uncontrolled blood pressure, smoking, and stress.

For years I was frustrated with my mother. Why wouldn't she use all of her God-given talents? Instead, she hid in her house and avoided the world.

As I continued to work in the world of mental health, I found empathy for my mother and stopped fighting. The last few years were better but not great. I was glad when I discovered my mother was dying. I wouldn't have to worry about clearing the air between us. We had our understanding and now we would just spend time together until she passed on to the next plane of existence.

My mother had always said that when she died and got her new body she would have long legs and red hair and know how to play the saxophone. This is how I imagine her now—and giving the angels hell, of course.

CHAPTER 9

Kited Kintanda—The Governor of the Country

STARTING IN THE 1990S, MY father would proudly announce that he was African American. This has always raised a few eyebrows since he was Caucasian and didn't have a South African accent. However, he was born and raised in Africa. Now known as the Democratic Republic of the Congo, the Belgian Congo was the place where my grandfather Olavi set up his medical missionary practice. My father spent the first ten years of his life in the village of Songa. After the first ten years, the family traveled back and forth between Africa and America for an additional ten-plus years. My father was given an African name by the tribespeople: Kitadi Kantanda, the governor of the country, due to the quiet and brave manner in which he carried himself. He was well named.

My childhood memories of Thanksgiving and Christmas consist of food, gifts, and eight-millimeter films of Africa. My grandfather narrated slide shows and films of the family trips and daily life in Africa. My grandfather couldn't be bothered to edit the films or organize the slides so one minute we were looking at the family talking and playing with one another, the children hamming it up for the camera, the African tribesman in their daily life, and then you would get a picture or moving picture of a tribesman with an enormous goiter that would impede his ability to get around. I was always struck by how happy the people were in front of the camera. Their big smiles became even larger as they posed for their before pictures and prepped for surgery, excited to be rid of the physical hardship the goiters caused them. We watched them prep for surgery, showing their disfigurements; sometimes my grandfather would have someone film a surgery and then we would see the post-op results. They would hold up the goiter, victoriously, like a conquered monster. It was always amazing. I never grew tired of these films, seeing my father and his family in another time and place, helping people who needed and wanted the help. All were very happy, or so it seemed anyway—my grandfather's propaganda.

My grandfather has his own interesting story that he documented in his book, *They Called Me Bwana Munanga*. My grandfather was born and raised in Finland. My grandfather's family chose to be baptized Seventh Day Adventists, starting the first SDA church in their hometown of Savonlinna, Finland. They were among four hundred Seventh Day Adventists in the entire country. The family, like all families in Finland, were also greatly affected by the Swedish/Finnish War and the conflicts that occurred in World War I and II. After a scholastic trip in Sweden, my grandfather decided to change the family name from Rosenberg to Rouhe, to reflect his Finnish heritage and not be mistaken for a Swede. This name change caused conflict in the family and not everyone fell in line. I have extended family that have gone back to the original name as a result. The trip to Sweden also influenced his decision to become a doctor after he heard about all the good they were doing in Africa. He wanted his life to make a difference, so he traveled to the United States and attend the newly opened SDA medical school at Loma Linda Medical University in Loma Linda, California.

He was part of one of the first graduating classes from Loma Linda and we now have three generations of Rouhe family members who have become medical doctors through Loma Linda. My grandfather met my grandmother, who was training to be a nurse at a nearby SDA college and also had a passion for missionary work. They married the day my grandfather received his certification of completion of medical studies.

They spent their early careers in Glendale, California, working to gain enough experience to qualify for missionary work. They traveled back to Finland to visit family and work on getting sponsors for an African mission. My grandfather got permission to study tropical medicine in Belgium. As my grandparents prepared for their first trip to Africa, they were waiting for all the paperwork to go through in England. This was fortunate for my grandmother, who gave birth to her first child at the Royal Hospital in London.

In 1937, the young family arrived in Songa, a mission site for the SDAs since 1921. The site consisted of the village, a twelve-bed hospital, and the missionary house. My grandmother had her second and third sons in Africa, my uncle Richard and my father. They spent a couple of years in Northern California, where my aunt Suzanne was born, and then headed back to Sonja, where, eight months later, the last son, Lyndon, was born. The family spent a significant amount of time in Africa. My uncles Ed and Richard, the two oldest, took a train to the southern part of the continent to attend school and came home on school holidays. The family had an adventurous life.

All of the siblings have their African artifacts as tokens of their life in the village. When the children were older my grandmother wanted them to receive an American education. She took the children and moved to Husen, California. My grandfather would travel between Husen and Sanga for a few more years, adding other mission trips in between Sanga visits to broaden his work.

The three older boys became the real version of *American Graffiti*, a great film set in the 1950s about coming of age in a small town and the cars that influenced them. The boys loved cars. This affection/affliction started when they were children in Africa. One of my favorite photographs is of the kids standing in a line with their cars in tow. The car fascination stayed with them when they moved back to the United States. It was the perfect time to be an adolescent who loved cars. The advent of the hot rod shaped their lives.

My father and his brothers have many stories about buying and fixing up their cars, racing other boys, and courting girls in their new rides. When they weren't going to school or working on their cars they were working in the orchards picking produce or cleaning dog kennels, anything to make extra money for their auto hobby. My father and his older brothers maintained their love of cars throughout their lives and have owed many vehicles among the three of them.

My father went back and forth to Africa as a teenager and young man to help his father. During his senior year of high school he spent time at Neubold College to keep up his schooling while his parents were in Africa. His uncle was the dean of the school and kept an eye on Stanley while the family was on mission. At this point, my father's older brothers were already in college, his sister was in high school staying with family in California and Lyndon, the youngest, was in his own special school starting at the age of seven.

He went to a special school for mentally handicapped children. Cave Springs was a family owned and operated SDA school; he was well cared for and spent most of his life there working on the property and living with friends on-site. It was a difficult decision for my grandparents to make, but given their missionary lifestyle and all their travels, it was better for Lyndon to have a consistent daily routine.

My father was eleven when he and his parents took Lyndon to Cave Springs for the first time. It was difficult for my father to understand why they had to leave his brother. Lyndon was upset on the day they left. Their parting left an indelible mark on my father. My grandfather was very pragmatic and emotionally distant so he could move on, but my grandmother was conflicted, and it was this conflict my father responded to the most. He used all this angst as his justification for bringing Lyndon to our home in the late 1990s, a decision that would dramatically change his life for the better.

Once my father completed high school in California, he went back to Neubold. This was when he met my mother. On their first winter break, my father didn't have money to visit his family in the United States so he was going to stay at Neubold. My father and a friend of his took my mother to the train station. She was going to visit her French relatives for the winter break. At the last minute she asked him to go with her so he and his friend jumped on the train…with no passport and barely any money. When they arrived, he and his friend realized their circumstance and were further chagrined when they found they had no place to stay.

Paris for Christmas

My mother's family was not about to host these brazen young men. So they wandered the streets of Paris, sightseeing and nibbling on baguettes. My father saw my mother each day for thirty minutes in the parlor of my great-aunt and -uncle's apartment. My father and his friend slept on benches and just made the most of their time. As a Christmas gift my mother was given money. She chose to take my father to Maxim's, a famous five-star restaurant. She didn't realize my father had not eaten much or that he had nowhere to stay, so when they had their fine dining experience, complete with a wait staff who shadowed their every move, an expensive meal with very little food served, my father was not as appreciative as she would have liked. It was then he told her that he and his friend had been sleeping on benches and eating baguettes.

He said he left hungrier than when he had sat down but, of course, he was happy to spend time with my mother so he never complained. They talked about this story many times since, as youthful foolishness, my mother so embarrassed she had taken him there, not knowing it would have been so much better to go to a little diner where he could have a proper meal. Her fantasy clashed with his reality—a very common occurrence in their relationship.

My grandmother wanted my father to become a pastor. Her two oldest sons were both training to become doctors and she wanted a pastor in the family. My father was always more sensitive in nature in comparison to the family. He was quiet and introspective. My grandmother thought the world of medicine would be too hard on him; ministry was a better fit. My father continued his training at Southern Missionary College (now Southern Adventist College), where he discovered ministry was not his calling. This decision came after his first sermon. My mother was sitting in the front row supporting her then boyfriend as he droned on and on and on. She said she actually heard a few people snoring. He was not a gifted public speaker and his need for people to take things seriously made him a little too preachy. They both agreed he needed to change his focus. He had always had an interest in medicine, so he changed his major and worked hard to complete his prerequisites for medical school within the remaining two years.

When my father asked my mother to marry him, my mother and her family were so excited. In the SDA community, the Rouhe family had a great reputation for being hard workers and dedicated to missions, a revered service in the SDA world. My Swedish grandparents gladly consented. It was important to my mother that her father be the one to marry them, and since my father was used to traveling, he was happy to have the wedding in Sweden. My father had three attendants: his brother Richard, close friend and fellow Paris wanderer, and my mother's brother Torgny.

Torgny decided to play a trick on my mother and sat on his top hat prior to the wedding. She panicked until he stood up proudly and popped it back open again unscathed. She was furious but too happy to hold a grudge. She did enjoy retelling the story for many years, though. My mother's three attendants included her closest friends. It was a traditional Swedish wedding. My parents were married by a justice of the peace on Friday, then held a church wedding on Saturday and a sending off on Sunday. After their honeymoon they returned to California to complete their degrees.

My father followed in his father's and brother's footsteps, attending Loma Linda Medical School from 1964 through 1969. While he was working on his rotations he considered three different specialties: psychiatry, neurosurgery, and infectious disease. He ultimately found that neurosurgery was the best fit since it was a challenge he enjoyed. He greatly enjoyed his residency and worked side jobs at other hospital emergency rooms to make extra money. He and my mother would take trips in their small Carmengia with their dogs: an Afghan hound and a poodle. This little troop saw a lot of Southern California in these days.

After eight years of marriage, I was born. As soon as I could travel, I, too, followed along on these excursions. My father finished his residency in 1974 and completed his boards the same year. He continued working at Loma Linda and various other jobs including as a pit medic for the Riverside Raceway. I went with him a few times and absolutely fell in love with the sights and sounds. I, too, caught the car bug.

My father received an opportunity to complete a six-month fellowship in London, England, in 1978. I was in the first grade. I attended a small private elementary school run by an English headmaster. My parents worked out a school schedule with her and my teacher to maintain my schooling while I was in England. I also attended school in England. It was a great experience. My parents brought my Great-Aunt Helen to act as my nanny and to include her in our family adventure. I love my Aunt Helen. She and I got along famously. She loved animals, and we would take many walks to Hyde Park to see the swans in the lake or the horse on the trails. We went to the Buckingham Palace stables to visit the horses and spent time at the London Zoo. On the weekends, we would take road trips to Wales or Scotland or just wander the English countryside.

LONDON TO AUTOBAHN AND BACK

My father decided to treat himself to his first Mercedes at the beginning of this trip. He, my Aunt Helen, and I went to Germany to pick up the car. When he drove it off the factory lot he spun out trying to get on the freeway. I will never forget my Aunt Helen's face. She was delighted and a little concerned about what she had just gotten herself into. My mother was in France visiting her family so she missed out on this experience.

While in London, my parents rented a flat and for the only time in my life, I got a feel for city living, complete with double-decker buses plus the underground trains. It was a great adventure. Once my father completed his fellowship, we went to Sweden to spend time with my mother's family and her lifelong friends. We returned late that summer and I went back to my little life that fall.

My father started his private practice that fall (1978). He had an office in the same building until he retired in 2003. When he started he had two women to manage his office and they stayed with him until my mother took over in 1990. My father was a successful surgeon. He always worked with at least one other neurosurgeon even though they had separate practices. They believed in a team effort when it came to surgery. It was rare for him to not have an assistant or for him to not assist in surgery.

He practiced new techniques with a fellow surgeon who kept mice for this purpose. I spent many an evening getting mice prepped for surgery and acting as recovery nurse in post op. My father was a fast, efficient surgeon. The less time spent under anesthesia, the better the results; this helped his patients recover faster after surgery. He operated both on the brain and the spine. He was best known for alleviating terrible back problems. He had a busy practice for twenty-five years. He loved the work and his patients.

While he was practicing medicine, he came home around seven in the evening, had dinner, and then worked on furniture kits until midnight. He loved to sand down the materials and mix stains for the furniture he ordered in unassembled kits. It was a great stress relief for him to work with his hands. It was crafty, albeit risky behavior (given that he could damage his hands doing this work), which was my mother's biggest concern. Our family home was filled with furniture that my father made during this time. He also enjoyed working in the garden. He gained these skills while living in Africa and working in the orchards in Husen. I enjoyed being outside with him, either working alongside him or, more likely, playing with my model horses creating ranches and herds.

An entertaining side note: "8:37"

Once when I was about ten years old I asked my dad what time he would be home that night, a common question. He said 8:37 (it was a surgery day). I went about my day and was tinkering in my room having completely forgotten about our conversation, assuming his statement was sarcasm, when I heard him come home, roar up the stairs, and down the hall to my room. He had a big smile on his face pointing to his watch. It read 8:37.

As my father became an established successful neurosurgeon he became financially successful. However, he was not comfortable with financial planning; he would rather just spend after the bills were paid. My mother was more financially savvy but got tired of the ongoing differences of opinion. He was a sucker for a good story and gave money away to anyone who won his heart. Since he was so successful this didn't hurt our family but it drove my mother crazy. As a way to counter this behavior she suggested making improvements to the house. So in the early 1980s they started on the property then made improvements to the driveway, added a two-story garage with four-car garage on top and a workshop below. They added a pool and pool house, chicken coop, and garden shed. But, like with many big projects, problems occurred and things were not always done according to plan. So this, too, ended up creating a lot of angst in our household. The work was completed in a few years—much later than the few months we had been told it would take. But we all breathed a sigh of relief when it was done. The next big financial investment was the horse ranch, and then I went to college.

During the 1980s there were people in the medical field who were taking advantage of the Medicare billing system. This set in motion insurance changes that ultimately changed how medicine was delivered in the United States. It dramatically changed private practitioners' ability to perform since now all procedures had to be approved by a third party. This changed the day-to-day operations of the office, the staff, and the profit margins. My father was frustrated by all these changes and asked my mother to help in the office. This proved to be a dramatic change for all involved and almost destroyed their marriage. I was glad I was away at college but sad to hear of the ongoing turmoil and sadder still when that turmoil added to already tense family vacations.

My father never really did learn how to financially plan. He did change his spending behavior but I would call it a white-knuckle change. It was out of necessity versus a real shift. Again my parents found another project to distract themselves: the house in Lake Arrowhead. This project was huge in the beginning, including lifting the foundation of one part of the house. The house projects were coming to a close when my mother went to Sweden to be with her dying father. I took over the financial management of the office and my parents' expenses. And a year later my father was diagnosed with stage three prostate cancer.

He minimized the diagnosis, saying he would do what was necessary and then going back to work. According to him, it was nothing to really worry about. I wanted my parents to organize their finances enough to establish a family trust and/or have a living will. Despite my well-founded arguments I was ignored and my mother was furious that I would even broach the subject. She felt I had ulterior motives for my request. Dealing with the loss of her father meant she had to start dealing with her parents' stuff. She felt as though everyone was behaving like a bunch of vultures. She didn't want to discuss who was getting what when he died. So planning for my parents' deaths was just killing her father all over again. Unspeakable…there was no winning this argument.

When my dad went in for his surgery my mother and I went with him to the surgery prep area. It was surreal to see him in patient garb when I was so used to seeing him as the surgeon. During the surgery, my mother and I were in the waiting room. I had brought papers to read and she watched political shows on the TV. She chastised me for reading…how could I possibly concentrate with my father in surgery? For me surgery was a part of life: he was getting fixed; this was a good thing.

He came out of the surgery a withdrawn man. It was an extensive operation, changing his hormone levels completely since the cancer was testosterone responsive. He gained some weight and became more emotional due to the increased estrogen in his system. He would joke with me when he and my mother went out that the girls were going out. He would treat his messenger bag as a handbag. I had a good laugh but my mother was not nearly as amused. "Oh, Stanley!" she would say.

He recovered from the surgery and went back to work after about a month. It helped him to work and he was more appreciative of his patients' own recovery processes. But he still felt like something was missing.

My father was raised SDA and fell away from the church while in college. Both he and my mother were SDA black sheep, rebels in the beliefs and cultures of the churches they were raised in. Now, having faced a major health concern, he was feeling the need to get back in touch with his spirituality. He went back to church and reading the Bible.

He did this with his youngest brother, Lyndon, who now lived in a group home near the rest of the family in Riverside, California. Both of my father's older brothers had settled in Riverside after medical school. Their parents moved to Riverside in the 1990s from Northern California to be near the boys. My Aunt Suzanne lives in San Luis Obispo, just a few hours away. So it made sense to move Lyndon from his longtime home of Cave Springs, Tennessee, to Riverside, California.

My dad was glad to have more time with Lyndon. Lyndon loved church. He listened to sermons and Christian music with his headphones and Walkman. Since my dad was spending more time with Lyndon, it was natural for him to go back to church because that is what Lyndon wanted to do. But my father could not go back without asking questions. This became his new hobby. He bought hundreds of books (I'm not kidding) and researched his questions in various concordances, cross-referencing his concerns with other religions to try to discover answers. He spoke to the pastor and engaged in intense debates with my mother. My parents loved to discuss their concerns and would give each other reading materials to add to their discussions.

My father's spiritual life became a source of new hope. He decided that whatever problems he had with the SDA church could be addressed and changed. He sought to get others to feel the same way. He went to a local group of former Adventists to recruit them to his cause. Instead, he joined their cause and became a regular attendant of the Trinity Community Church and a former Adventist. He continued to take Lyndon to church until Lyndon passed away from congenital heart failure. He was 58 years old, amazing for someone with Down syndrome.

Lyndon's death and my father's recent conversion to evangelical Christianity gave him new passion. He went back to his pastoral roots and began preaching to anyone who would listen. His golf partners called their golf games "holy roller time." There were times when he became a bit unbearable. For example, when we ate out together, he would ask our waiter what their belief system was and would they like to talk about their stance on God. Or when he challenged my then boyfriend's (soon-to-be husband's) grandmother, a Christian Scientist, on why she didn't believe in God and why my father did not think she was saved. Oh boy, it was not fun. Needless to say, this also drove my mother crazy, and the group my father joined (the former Adventists) in her mind were to blame. Eventually, he did settle down; by the time he retired he was considering going back into the missionary field: less preaching, more doing—a mantra that suited him well and resonated with his family roots.

Retirement from the operating room was a welcome relief; he'd had a tough schedule and needed to slow down. Although his cancer had remained in remission now for almost ten years, which was a miracle in itself, he was getting older and just needed to slow down. But what ended up happening instead was a shifting of gears. He began investing in new business ventures.

His fleeting moment of living debt free was over. My father's previous affliction for being a sucker for a good story came true again, as he went through several years of poor property investments and several generations of medical equipment distributions companies.

Finally in 2008, he started a medical distribution company with people who worked with him instead of taking advantage of him and proved he had learned from his previous mistakes. He had a great team of people he had worked with over the years and finally had a successful venture, which only grew. He was recovering from his previous financial concerns and making real headway when he discovered he was dying from pancreatic cancer.

Since the time my father was diagnosed with prostate cancer he started to come to terms with his mortality. His decision to have Lyndon more actively involved in his life was a godsend both spiritually and emotionally. Their time together allowed my father to connect to his childhood and young adult memories and let go of some of the guilt he had for not spending more time with Lyndon when they were younger. I believe my father still had guilt about his family dynamic, as illustrated by an interview he gave just two weeks prior to his passing. This article caused quite a stir since it was filled with the author's agenda and my father's guilt and need to make sure everyone he cared about was saved from their sins.

FATHER'S DAY

My dad was a golfer. He had rebelled against this idea initially. He thought it was cliché and took too much time away from other projects. But eventually the location of our family home won out and he began to play. He and his friends would go on amazing trips to Scotland, Ireland, and Hawaii to play golf, sometimes fifty-four holes in one day. This was rare but it happened. My dad worked hard so he could play hard.

After the prostate cancer scare, he and I were spending more time together. I decided I would learn how to play. I took lessons, practiced, and quickly realized this was going to take a really long time to learn and too much of my precious free time. I started looking for alternatives.

I found Bondurant Racing School.

On Father's Day of 1998 I got a pedal car restored with the license plate "Stan's Toy," a mock race-car track with a finishing card saying we were going racing—a three-day Grand Prix course where we would learn some mad skills.

Dad and I have always shared the joy of cars. Everything car is a Rouhe tradition but he and I made it special for us. We enjoyed going to car shows and car museums and, of course, the racing was amazing. We ended up going back to Bondurant a few times over the years, and each time was filled with great memories. Yes, I beat him but only on the autocross—it turns out to be my specialty. He loved driving the small open-wheeled/Formula One types on the big track. I preferred learning maneuvers like J-turns, PIT, and controlled slides.

The sound of revving engines and speeding cars going by and the gleaming cars of the future at auto shows will forever bring a smile to my face and warm my heart.

In the end, Dad raced to the finish putting the pedal to the metal saying, "Come on, let's go!"

CHAPTER 10

Life Is Not a Punishment

I AM BLESSED WITH THE gift of faith. I never question God's presence. I have always felt a connection to Him. Even in my lowest times I have not felt forsaken. I have felt extremely frustrated and sad but I always knew the Lord would provide a way.

This became more solidified for me when I was going through my breakup and divorce. I was truly at my lowest emotional point and knew it was my connection with God that got me through, helping me place one foot in front of the other. He helped me leave my problems at the door so I could help others and thereby gain perspective on my own life, because somebody always has it harder or has a more heart-wrenching story than you.

Having said that, there is one experience I had during this time in my life that I would not wish upon anyone. Anyone.

ASHES TO ASHES

As I mentioned before, I used the same mortuary for both of my parents. Both of my parents' remains were cremated. The mortician informed my father and me when we met him in his office that he would contact us when my mother's ashes were ready to be picked up. He said it would take about two weeks.

When I went back to the mortuary after my father died I paid for his remains to be cremated. It was the next check to be written in the family checkbook. After my father had written a check for my mother's remains to be cremated, I wrote one for his…

The mortician informed me that my mother's remains were not ready yet. Well, frankly, neither was I, so I thanked him perhaps a bit too enthusiastically and left.

When I got back from my trip to Utah and felt somewhat more together I started working on my plan for what to do with my parents' stuff and packed for my trip to Sweden. That's when I got the call from the mortuary; one of my parents' ashes were ready and the death certificates were also in; could I come and pick them up? I arranged to do so the next day.

It turns out that both of my parents' remains were ready for pickup as well as their death certificates. I came to the mortuary alone. True to form, I had turned down the offer for help and walked out to the car with a box of ashes under each arm and two envelopes of death certificates. It was a death march. I realized halfway to my car that I would never wish this on anyone no matter how they had wronged me. A person should never have to experience this.

I didn't feel sorry for myself. I just took note of the absurdity of it all. In a way it was very telling of my perceived role in the family. I carry the important things and now it's my responsibility to see them to their resting place. I am not being punished for surviving my parents. Who else could step in and take care of this situation? I was being given what I could handle. I now know I can handle a lot!

By now, I think it is clear how much I love stories.

I love learning about the different characters, understanding their strengths, the challenges of figuring out who I'm going to cheer for, and wondering how it is all going to work out. I enjoy the journey; it is why I became a therapist—that and my parents' refusal to listen to me. So why not go help people who actually seek you out for help?

I knew working as a therapist would be rewarding. But I could not have predicted how life-changing some of my clients would be for me. There are moments with clients I will always remember. I have truly enjoyed walking with people as they work through their personal roadblocks and change their lives.

Of course, I have a lot of entertaining stories of circumstances I have been through, into, or had to work my way out of. The stories that stand out to me now are the ones in which I have watched a person face their fears, connect to their spirituality, and truly change their life. They acknowledge the good, the bad, and the ugly. They seek to repair the damage done where it is possible and they live their lives always seeking to be better than they were the day before.

Before my parents passed away I had lost people close to me: grandparents, a parent of a good friend in high school, but I had not felt it as personally as I did when I had the following session with a client I was working with in a residential treatment center.

A Client Teaching Me about Loss

I was working with a woman in her seventies who struggled with alcohol dependency. Her husband was in poor health and she wanted to get better so she could be there for him in his last days. She had been in the program for about thirty to forty-five days when she started to get antsy and wanted to go home to see her family and be with her husband. This is a typical response for anyone new in recovery and research has shown the success rate of a person struggling with addiction who seeks treatment dramatically improves if they stay in treatment for ninety days or more. Anything less than that and they are likely to slip back into their old ways since they have not had enough time to identify all of their personal obstacles.

But given her family circumstances, I was torn about what to recommend, and so we discussed the options. Her son was planning a visit and we were going to have a family session to discuss his concerns and make a decision. The day before he was due to arrive he called me and said that his father had passed away the night before. He wanted to wait to tell his mother in person and asked if we could do this during session. I agreed. I will never forget that session.

Her mournful wail said more than words could ever express. This was true, deep-seated grief and I felt very honored and saddened to be a witness to this pain. We spent the rest of her treatment reconciling the death of her husband while she was in treatment and how she would continue to care for herself when she returned home, identifying what would be her new motivation for recovery. As with most of my clients, I don't know the end to her story but I carry her in my heart and wish her well.

It was this session that came to my mind the summer when my parents passed away. The pain I felt I had seen before; this was to be expected and someday I would feel differently. I would heal.

Since I believe life is a gift, not a punishment, I chose to focus on what I could learn about myself, my parents, my family, and my friends through this shift in my life. I wanted to find meaning but I didn't want to create it. So while I sorted through my parents' physical lives I reflected on my own.

I believe my wondering path prepared me to come out of these circumstances stronger than I was when I came into them. My work in my father's office and managing my parents' finances allowed me to take them over relatively easy and navigate their somewhat chaotic, if not extremely frustrating, financial waters with relative ease.

My work as a teacher and later as a cognitive psychologist gave me a unique perspective as a therapist. It allowed me to take leadership positions, to teach others, create curriculums, and develop new programs. My openness and curiosity in wanting to understand a person's perception allowed me to work without fear or apprehension with people who struggled with serious mental illness. My clients inspired me to be a better person, to look at my own life, to be accountable, and to become stronger.

So when it came time to be there for my parents and to sit with them as they left this world, I could imagine no other place I would rather have been. I was grateful we had come to terms with our differences and this time could be spent just connecting and loving each other. It was also important to allow other people to have their connection and to help them feel welcome to connect. I have grown as a person through the loss of my parents and seek to find what is next in my life without forcing my agenda.

CHAPTER 11

Daydreaming...

MY IMAGINATION HAS SERVED ME well. It has proven itself to be a great distraction in hard times and provided plenty of entertaining stories when I was young, perhaps even a unique perspective on life, but the downside to distraction is avoidance to the point of unconscious awareness. In the therapy world, this would be the distinction between survival skills and defensive mechanisms.

There are twelve identified defensive mechanisms that have been categorized through years of observation and provide an expected reaction formation to each identified defense mechanism. This is all a fancy way of discussing judgment. Yes, it is true we are each unique, but it turns out our response to circumstances can often be categorized into patterns that often stem from similar circumstances. Our responses can be predicted to a certain extent. The purpose of understanding the pattern from a clinical standpoint is to "buck the system," create productive challenges to encourage personal reflection, awareness, shift in thought process, and change in behavior.

A survival skill can be either mental, physical, or spiritual and is often very specific to the individual's environment. It is important for a therapist to help their client understand their defensive mechanism(s) so the benefits and the drawbacks for these skills can be determined. Every skill and/or mechanism has positive and negative qualities. Understanding these qualities allows a person to make conscious choices about their behaviors and thereby break cycles in order to change behavior.

As a child, I had invisible friends. Some were pure products of my imagination and others were inspired by current television shows. My regular friend was Marcia from *The Brady Bunch* television show. My mother was concerned until her research indicated that children with imaginary friends are often very bright and use this form of imagination to stretch their brain power, or they are psychotic. She went with the first option. She was right: I'm not psychotic, although I wasn't always sure that was the case, but more on that later.

It is more common for only children to have imaginary friends, but all children can create them as an outlet for emotions, conversation, comfort. My Uncle Lyndon had "Feely." Feely stayed with Lyndon his whole life. Feely was his conscious and spiritual guide. Feely would challenge Lyndon when he was misbehaving and he would comfort Lyndon when he was distressed. Lyndon would sometimes spend hours in his room talking to Feely to work things out. Every time he came out of his room, he felt better and knew what to do. I'll admit there were a few times when I was a kid and then later on when Lyndon lived with my parents that I would stand outside his door and listen for a little while. Feely was a great counterpart to Lyndon and I was impressed with how he used this relationship to improve himself.

No offense to Marcia Brady, but I don't think she changed me for the better. I did feel comforted by having someone to talk to and share in adventures. It was nice to have a buddy without any drama. As I grew older—say, after the age of six—I would use my imagination to come up with stories, adventures. These adventures started when I was younger and would play with my model horses. Then, once I had real horses, I would use them as a part of my adventure. We would solve mysteries together and save people from a burning building or some other perilous situation. We were a team, heroes out to save the world. As a young teenager, boys were substituted for horses.

FULL CIRCLE

The daydream adventures proved to be a great escape for stressful times. I would daydream my problems away and therefore never really face them either. This became more true after the sixth grade, when I decided to take a stand against a friend who I felt was behaving badly. I ended up being ostracized from our group with no one to play with or talk to. I was stubborn and knew I was right. Now they were all being bullied by her too. However, I had unfortunately done my fair share of rough play when I was younger to some of these very kids and had never really apologized. I felt as though maybe this was payback and I should take my medicine.

The aggression occurred when I was very young and I know now it was a result of not feeling like I was able to talk about or deal with my frustrated feelings so I took them out on my classmates. This was not OK and I did feel bad about it. As I grew older, I took my anger out on myself by stuffing my emotions with food and negative self-talk. Now that things had come to a boil, I wanted a chance to apologize, but the dynamic of the new ringleader being a child of a teacher at the school prevented me from going near the group. This lasted several weeks. My mother wanted to intervene but I said I wanted to handle it for myself.

When I was allowed to talk to them, I started with asking what happened: what had gone wrong? No one said anything, so I said this may or may not be relevant but I owe certain people an apology in this group and I apologized to each of them. Then I left. I never spoke to them again.

The principal decided to get involved. She tried to resolve the situation by talking to each of the students in our class and then to me. I told her I was willing to cooperate but the new ringleader wasn't going to win this power play. The principal was outmatched by a mother/daughter dynamo. I finished the year out and did not go to my sixth grade graduation, something I had been looking forward to since I had first started in the school in prekinder-garten and had watched my first graduation at the age of four. This was the price I was willing to pay because there was no going back. The relationships had been forever changed.

I did run into a few of the kids on separate occasions a couple of years later. They apologized right away, saying that any rough play I may have done when I was younger was mutual within the group and definitely did not warrant what had happened. When I asked what had happened to cause such a rift, they all had a similar embarrassed response and none of them really knew.

As an interesting side note, years later I recommended the school to a colleague new to the area. She went on a tour, told the principal who had recommended her, and the principal said to please have me come in and they would love to see me. The principal wanted to apologize for what had happened. I never did go to see them. I decided I didn't want to rehash the situation. But it was nice to have the apology. Now I regret not going to see them since it probably would have been much more for their benefit than mine. By not going they were deprived of that relief. Again, I'm sorry.

When I prepared to start seventh grade I thought I had learned my lessons and I was ready to move on to big, bad junior high and bigger, badder high school. Since my imagination was great, I could fake being tough. I told myself and anyone who would listen that I loved my life and everything was great! But inside I was miserable and felt unworthy of just about anything. I buried my emotions with food and with a nice padding of twenty to forty pounds I was safe from attention—the attention I was sure would lead to emotional pain. I was a self-imprisoned prisoner. I wanted the boys to pay attention to me, not just be my friend, but my physical barrier kept them at arm's length. I escaped through riding, studying, and daydreams.

My mother observed all of this and responded to the symptoms, not the underlying cause. She wanted me to see how special I was to her. In her eyes, I was bright, beautiful, and talented. I would nod, smile, and avoid her whenever these topics came up. This frustrated her when I ignored her accolades and instead seemed to make an effort to put on weight versus losing it. Our fights about weight and clothes took on real momentum.

I was miserable. I went through the motions of my day-to-day life. I was busy with my college prep studies, which had a high emphasis on science; my tennis and volleyball schedules; and riding/competing. I was nicely distracted when I wasn't fixated on my misery. I knew that I wanted to go to college and in the end I applied and got into two, USC and Westmont College. I chose Westmont because it had a prettier campus and I could imagine myself there better than in L.A. What I couldn't imagine was my life past the age of twenty-three.

I graduated from college when I was just twenty-one, but I really lost focus of what my life would look like or feel like after college. My goal of becoming a vet was smashed by pure intimidation of my competitors. Then I thought, OK, medical school. But between an adviser who told me I would be a better nurse than a doctor, the changes in medicine, and my father's reaction to the changes, I lost my motivation.

I graduated successfully with no further plan and then, to add insult to injury, I had a bad riding accident two weeks after graduation and ended up in the hospital for two and a half days. I eventually got back on my feet, back in the saddle, and went from working in my dad's office to teaching high school to being a graduate student to meeting my future husband.

I married potential, not reality. Oh, the sting. All those negative self-thoughts and beliefs never really went away; they just went dormant. They went full steam when I met my now ex-husband. He was a personal trainer and a fun-loving guy, or so I thought—two things I enjoyed on paper but not in reality. I was too intimidated by his physical fitness, which I translated to a superior sense of self over my own self-doubt and neurosis. I decided to face my fears, which I think was good for me. But I should have gotten out of the relationship after six to eight months, not eight to ten years.

However, this relationship made me face all my worst nightmares and brought me to my emotional and spiritual knees. I was humbled in ways I didn't know were possible. I discovered my biggest fear was that I would be left alone and have no family. Once I voiced that fear, I found connections in friends and strengthened my spiritual life. I found I could face this fear and let go of this negative relationship. I now feel that was the hardest thing I have ever done and it prepared me for my life in 2011.

While I was going through all this emotional crap, I found that Disneyland was a good distraction. I lived close by and I had an annual pass. So it made it very easy for me to go and escape. I didn't have to think, be creative, or do anything other than let the "Disney imagineers" do their work. I wandered the parks and immersed myself in the distraction of it all. So it's not strange to me that after my father died I wanted to go somewhere familiar and just escape.

Both of my parents were avid readers, my mother especially. Stories were their way of escape. One thing we could always do together was go to the movies. The movie would provide another world to explore and all the family angst would just go away.

Books also provided an escape, something my parents and I shared together. They would discuss current events, research topics in literature, read contemporary novels and nonfiction to add food to their fodder. Most people didn't stand a chance in a debate. Between these two powerhouses, they were armed and ready to fight—I mean discuss.

My mother discovered this talent when she was very young. She and her father would discuss topics in the news or in books or even in the Bible as their bonding time. My mother continued this tradition with my father and she loved him for it. My mother loved thinking about things and theorizing much more than actual living—ugh, that was for peasants was her take on things. I always marveled at this phenomenon and struggled to understand it or describe it to other people until I saw the movie *The Adventures of Baron Von Munchausen.*

The Moon King

In the story, the baron must go on various adventures to collect and reunite his team of desperadoes to help a young girl in need. One of these adventures takes him to the moon to negotiate with the king. Both the king and the queen of the moon have the unique ability to separate their heads from their bodies. They have what appear to be Elizabethan-like collars made up of two parts, one attached to the neck connected to the head and one attached to the neck connected to the body. They could separate if the body used its arms to spin the head off or if the head twisted itself violently enough to dislodge. Once separated the head could float and maneuver on its own. Use your imagination or rent the movie. Robin Williams played the king of the moon, and when he first discovered the baron, he was annoyed by the interruption. He was busy "creating things using his imagination." He later discussed his revolution to his body because all it wanted to do was eat, fart, and have sex. These bodily functions disgusted him. His head worked very hard to avoid his body, which managed to catch him (the head) with a butterfly net.

Imagination people, it's great fun. Once I saw this scene, I thought, *finally, a way to describe and understand my mother*! She worked very hard to avoid her body, and I think ultimately she was glad to be rid of it.

The day after my father's death I didn't want to stay at home. I didn't want to be alone. I didn't want to see family or friends. I just wanted to wander. Randy and I went to Disneyland.

Now, if you have a macabre sense of humor, you might say, "Hey there, what do you do when your parents pass away? Go to Disneyland!"

This wasn't to have fun, however. It was to distract my emotionally, physically, and spiritually overloaded self. The only thing I remember from the day was driving there (Randy drove) and thinking *this is going to sound really bad when people hear this later.* I remember having to go to the admission kiosk to renew my annual pass since it had expired at the end of May. I remember walking into the park. That's it.

What resonated with me most throughout the first month after my parents passed away is that life goes on. People go to work, new movies get released, the world continues to spin on its axis. Not that my parents were these extremely important people and the world should stop and take notice. Rather the contrary, our lives are small and we need to appreciate them and do the most with what we have because someday we will be gone and the world will continue.

It raises the question: What kind of legacy do you want to leave behind?

CHAPTER 12

Why?

⤸

I LOVE ASKING "WHY?" ITS simplicity makes it a great question. It is the basis for our ability to learn and to grow, but sometimes I do it just to be annoying. For example, when I found myself on a miserable blind date during my third year of college, I asked why about anything and everything I could think of. The result? A "birthday cake" complete with a "Happy Birthday" song at the restaurant in an effort to embarrass me. Instead, I laughed it off and enjoyed the free cake, while I thought to myself...amateurs! Plus, now I had another funny story for the future. My friend who set up the date was not amused. I figured I had done her a favor. They were both idiots (as my mother would say).

As the only child of a neurosurgeon and a jurist doctorate I was gifted with a natural curiosity and intelligence. I asked why about things I wanted to truly understand. Both of my parents enjoyed discussing/debating topics, typically the more taboo the better...religion, politics, personal decisions. But they enjoyed intellectual discussions on any topic.

Now, an intellectual discussion is different from a typical discussion in which people just throw out their thoughts and oftentimes their emotional reactions to a topic and then try to pass it off as fact or even the deciding factor of said debate. Instead, an intellectual discussion is backed by knowledge. Both of my parents were eternal students. They loved to learn and I remember my mother seeking out her Encyclopaedia Britannica on many occasions to research a point she was trying to make. When I was a child they would answer my questions and we would discuss the topic in a student-teacher format. But once I started going to school I was encouraged to research the questions I had for them and then return with the answer so we could discuss it. At times this dissuaded my need to ask why because I wasn't so interested that I wanted to research the answer. However, most of the time I enjoyed these discussions. We filled many an evening during commercial breaks or during dinner with these talks.

When I started my master's in psychology (MFT), I was told within the first semester that I should NOT ask a client why they did something. Instead, I should seek to understand what were their motivations, internal dialogue, circumstances of the situation they are recounting, dynamics of the relationship that is being discussed, and so on. All of this made perfect sense and I certainly did all of those things. But I still asked why...not all the time, but once I established a rapport with a client there were times when I couldn't help but ask why. Why did you respond that way? Why do you think that about yourself? Why do you allow others to treat you one way when you wouldn't let someone else be treated that way? Why?

To ask why is to ask a purposely open-ended question, to allow for all associations or feelings that come to mind. In cognitive psychology we learn how people process information and then use the information to navigate their world. We learn through association. So as any psychodynamic or analyst will tell you, you learn the most about a person through their free associations. How they connect the dots in their mind tells you what is associated with each dot and how each dot relates to the others. The associations are anything from memories of certain events to facts or other sensations such as smell, touch, sound. To ask a person why allows for the truest response to the question.

Now, once you ask why you have to be open to all this information and have a willingness to consider each piece as you go through it. This allows the person who provided the free association to understand how to weigh each of these associations in level of importance and also understand how they themselves process information. This is why I find the process of mental illness so interesting. When a person is experiencing a psychotic moment, i.e., delusion or hallucination, it is a real sensation input to them that now needs a response based on their associations to that stimulus. To question the input is a waste of time. To help them work through their associations is always more effective.

Typically, people pull away from someone in a psychotic state, but it is better to engage and help them work through their process. This assumes you are safe and that their associations are not violent in nature. It is also important to encourage people to take their antipsychotic medications because these medications allow a person to experience these events and process them. Antipsychotics do not take the stimulus away; they just allow the process to occur.

What is the difference between psychosis and talking or acting crazy? I spoke a little bit about this in the introduction. Just to be clear, psychosis is a result of a hallucination and/or a delusion and can last as long as a day event or be a lifelong experience. Crazy is a response to circumstances that feel out of a person's control and their need to get them in their control. Oftentimes people know they are acting crazy but their need to make things right (not crazy-feeling) overrides their not wanting to be crazy in the moment. When you hear people describe *crazy* you will hear statements like, "I feel crazy, on edge, overwhelmed, out of my mind, my thoughts are racing, I can't focus, I just want this to stop." Crazy is a state of mind in which the question why cannot be answered or the answer does not compute.

FEELING CRAZY

I first started feeling crazy when I was a small child, let's say around three. My mother had a college friend who, I found out later in my life, had changed her name, changed her hair and lost a hundred pounds after the birth of her first child. Can we say postpartum depression? Her son was a few years older than me and when I was around three I began to feel uncomfortable around him.

Now I understand at this age I was just starting to gain my ability to remember and truly associate sensations with memories, but I have pictures that show a shift in my expression before the age of three and after when I was around this person. I was visibly stressed. This person wanted my attention all the time and it became tiring very quickly. Since our mothers were friends, I had no choice in the matter. I tried to play by myself but he would not allow that for long. His need for control and determination to have me next to him at all times began to take a toll on me as the years went on.

I dreaded seeing them in their home where the behavior was the worst. His behavior lessened in neutral areas or at our home so it was more tolerable. I expressed my concerns over the years but my mother did not understand. Eventually, my mother's friend got a divorce and moved to another, much more expensive, part of Southern California and there the crazy feeling sky-rocketed. Whatever was going on in that family dynamic seemed to hit me like a ton of bricks whenever we went to visit them.

I became very frustrated with my mother for forcing me into this situation time after time. I finally refused to go and got my father involved to say I could stay at home if my mother wanted to go visit this person. But this was after years of dealing with the situation so my reaction to tense, exhausting situations was well established. I withdrew into my daydreams, my playtime with my animals. I didn't want to spend time with a lot of people; it felt overwhelming and unsafe. Once I was away from this situation for a while I became more social and competing horses, riding with kids my own age, certainly helped get me out of my shell. But the survival skill of avoiding took its toll.

I now understand that my mother wanted to visit this friend because she was a connection to her past. This person was also European and their camaraderie was apparent whenever they got together. As I mentioned before my parents were not psychologically minded so connecting to my overwhelmed feelings due to lack of emotional space was a foreign concept and it took them a while to acclimate. I don't believe my mother was intentionally harming me by keeping me in a situation I was uncomfortable in. Once she realized how serious I was she listened to my concerns and stopped taking me with her on these visits.

I certainly had my share of crazy moments as a teenager and in my twenties. But the next time I really felt crazy was when I realized my ex was really not good for me. No matter what he said this relationship was destructive and it would destroy me if I stayed in it. My problem was that at this point, we had been together for nine years and my mother had told me he was not good for me for eight of those years. I didn't want to believe that she was right, that all this time had gone by, and I refused to see what was so obvious to so many other people. I avoided the truth until I almost lost my mind.

My refusal to see the relationship as destructive to me almost cost me my sanity. I wanted to have my own little family so badly I refused to get out and therefore denied to myself what was so evident to everyone else. When a person refuses to acknowledge information the disparity creates a mental rift in our processing. Allow this to go on and it will eventually lead to a major blow-up or breakdown. In order to heal we must face our truths. I had to ask myself why.

Why had I entered into this relationship in the first place? What purpose did it serve? Why did I stay in the relationship when there were obvious signs of incompatibility? What was going on with me that this disparity was OK and oftentimes welcomed as a distraction from my family (my parents)? These were really tough questions to answer and despite years of therapy it took me a really long time to face the truth because my skill of avoidance was entrenched. This was the hardest time of my life and I think it took a good two years of hard work, and an additional two more years of continued soul-searching to answer these questions and to face these truths.

The most painful truth was that I had to realize this despite all my intelligence and professional know-how. I had to burn my hand to a crisp to discover my insecurities. I had to go through all I went through emotionally, mentally, and spiritually in order to learn how to better care for myself.

When I told my mother I had no regrets she was appalled. She was furious, in fact, because she didn't understand how could I have put her through so much agony for so long and not regret my actions. I actually laughed at this statement and realized on a whole new level that even though I knew my mother loved me, life for her, at this point anyway, was all about how it affected her. I had to accept my mother for who she was…not who I wanted her to be. Then our relationship would be less tense and we could spend time together. I'm grateful I worked this out when I did because her health started to take a real turn for the worse six months later.

As much as I love to ask why and to understand things, I also know most big-picture questions I am not meant to understand in my human form. So in times of crisis, I don't bother asking why...I just do and die. I love that last phrase because for someone who comes from a thinking/analyzing family sometimes you just need to do and die, get out of the way and get the job done. My father and I were similar in this way, we are worker bees. We are/ were happy to have a job and work through the task. My mother, on the other hand, did not enjoy the day-to-day grind of a job or anything else for that matter. She preferred to muse on intellectual concepts or do short-term work. She was great in a crisis.

So as my mother's health became more of a concern, my father and I would discuss the best way to support her. He wanted to make her go to the doctor, make her take her medications, make her get better and enjoy life. My stance was you know better than to think you can make anyone do anything, especially Mom. He would eventually agree and then within days go right back to fighting with her because she wasn't doing what he had told her to do. This was our family dynamic for the last fifteen years of my parents' lives and defined their lives during the last three years.

When my mother's health really became a concern in August of 2010, I started to feel that she would not live to see another year. At first I kept this to myself, but after her first hospitalization, I told close friends. It's one thing to have a feeling about something; it's another thing to have the feeling come true. I also knew that if one of my parents died, the other would soon follow. They were so bonded to each other. They needed the push-pull of their relationship. It defined them in ways they could not see but I'm sure on some unconscious level they felt it.

However, I could not have predicted my father would die so soon after my mother. I was thinking they would be a least a few years apart. After all, they were so young. But then once my father told me his diagnosis I knew this was the end for both of them, and Mom was going first. So the events of 2011 were not a surprise to me; it did not require intense soul-searching or a need to ask why.

Instead, it was about loose ends, managing my parents' affairs, dealing with their stuff, and facing a life on this Earth without having to worry about either one of them. I had not realized how much time and energy I spent on this task. I worried about them a lot, and letting them go physically allowed me to connect to them mentally in a much more comforting way. I wanted to know their stories and tell them to other people. I wanted to ask questions and remember things others had told me about my parents.

So unlike most people I know or most books I have read about major loss and the grieving process, I did not need to ask why. I just wanted to acknowledge the truth: the truth of their relationship, the truth of their lives, and the truth of their legacies.

CHAPTER 13

Grief Is a Funny Thing

LIKE ALL EMOTIONS, GRIEF HAS its predictable nature. Emotions can be predictable. We count on it as therapists and spend our professional lives educating and guiding our clients through their emotional arcs. So as a therapist, I was prepared for the road ahead as I saw my mother's health rapidly declining and my father preparing to join her. What I did not count on, ironically, is my innate sense to react to things differently from most people.

As a child, I learned quickly my emotional reactions although within range were not typical. I was labeled quiet and reserved. As I grew up, that changed to awkward and entertaining. Not much has changed in me or those around me. My reactions polarize people; they either love me or hate me. I've accepted this while working to understand why I react the way I do, and I work to normalize myself when possible. I've been successful, for the most part. However, all this loss in such a short amount of time was too much for my internal emotional processor to handle and my grief response surprised me.

I predicted the endgame relatively quickly and so I started planning what needed to be done as a way of managing my overwhelming anxiety and grief. I was ridiculously busy for a solid six months after my parents passed and would become very upset at unpredictable times, manifesting itself in sobbing tears and martyrdom. These moments became less frequent and in time rare. But then the numbness settled in mixed with a real annoyance for everyone and everything. I was not prepared for this. I had expected to go through the five stages of grief—denial, anger, bargaining, depression, acceptance—but not like this!

The clinician in me tells me that our emotional process is never linear. We are working through stages by inhabiting one while dappling in those after and those before. So in any given moment my depression could manifest with flecks of anger, bargaining, and acceptance. What I wasn't prepared for was the apathy mixed with irritation. Here is a great example, which my friend and I can now have a good laugh at, but it still horrifies me on some level.

Take a Break or Not…

About seven months after my parents passed away I decided to slow down my full-court pressed on managing my parents' stuff and start focusing on my needs by getting some rest. I apparently embraced this with relish. My friend called me up and stated she was having a rough day…her life was legitimately very frustrating at the time and she would really like to go to the spa and take a break…was I game?

My response, you ask—you'd better sit down for this one. I replied I did not have any plans other than to sit down and do nothing. (Please read with a dry snotty tone.) And do you really want me to change my plans? Because if you want me to I guess I could meet you there (at the spa, where people go to relax and unwind). At the time, there was a small part of me in the recesses of my mind horrified with what came out of my mouth but the rest of me was saying, "You go, girl, you deserve to relax. Who needs to hear someone else's problems right now anyway?"

My friend (God bless her!) gave a little giggle then pulled it together and said, "No, no, you stay where you are; I'll be fine. We can talk later this week." I said OK, got off the phone, turned to my boyfriend, who managed at the last moment to pull his jaw back up to the general direction of his face, and I said, "I didn't want to go to the spa anyway!"

Clearly!

Who was this person? A friend calls in need, wants to go to the spa to relax, no talking really required, and I act like she invited me to clean Dumpsters for demolition…ridiculous! However, what really mystified me was how long I held onto this mind-set: days, with waves lasting months. I was tired of people. My perception of them was that they put their stuff on me and I had no tolerance left.

Of course, I've analyzed this and see the obvious frustration associated with my parents: not wanting to manage their lives and me being left holding the bag. I just wasn't prepared for the insidious nature of these feelings. My grief had infiltrated my life in ways I had no way of predicting, except to shrug and say, well, you know me…always different, always awkward. But I'm not OK with hurting others to benefit myself or because I can't be bothered to manage my own thoughts.

So where does redeveloping a filter and understanding your own thought process fit into the classic stages of grief? My guess is it is more reflective of the bigger grief. I lost my whole life perspective when my parents died. I had no one left to push against, be accountable to, to impress. I was on my own, left to carry the family legacy I knew would end with me and it scared me.

The other side of fear is anger. Each represents a reaction to circumstances that threaten us. My anger/fear was the embodiment of my grief and I had to identify it, recognize I'm prone to have these feelings again and again until one day I don't feel the need to snap at someone or get bent out of shape about really reasonable requests for me to change my plans.

Now I can go back to being entertained by my reactions and accountable to others when I go too far or not far enough. I accept myself and continue to strive to be better.

CHAPTER 14

Italian Greyhounds

EMOTIONAL MELTDOWNS SUCK.

This became an all too familiar feeling when I was facing my personal truth during the breakup of my first marriage. People tried to warn me I would likely act in ways that felt sensible at the time and then later, upon reflection, I would flinch recalling my actions. Well, sadly, I can say I started flinching from memories of my actions long before my divorce.

With age comes wisdom—oh yes, I can definitely say this is a true statement and what is worse is that sometimes you really don't even need that much time to pass for the wisdom to seep in. The trick is to give yourself the time to consider your actions and the potential consequences, to not force situations. Of course, you also have to understand when you're forcing something. I have found that when I get my mind set on something I develop tunnel-vision on the topic. Oftentimes, this means I am getting into forcing territory. In other words, when I get a little crazy about something, it's time for a time-out.

Case in point, October 2011.

I am knee-deep, literally, in my parents' stuff. They kept everything for fifty years, so when it came to figuring out what I was going to do with their stuff I soon realized I needed to have an estate sale or two. I spent two and half months going through fifty years' worth of stuff, sorting personal from valuable from important to sellable now, sellable later, donate, trash.

The first estate sale was the first weekend in November. I wanted to catch people during the holiday shopping season. Two weeks before the sale Randy and I were walking around a big mall and we went into a pet store to look at puppies. Just for fun, because they are cute. We saw two Italian Greyhound puppies roughhousing and stopped to watch them play for a while. They were very cute. We walked away. A week later I said to Randy, "Weren't those Italian Greyhound puppies cute? Wouldn't it be fun to have them?" and we started playing around with names: Bonnie and Clyde, Spencer and Tracy, Bogie and Bacall (my cousin had a pair of Dobermans with these names and I always thought they were clever names for a pair)…you get the idea.

Randy was sensing trouble but was playing along. Then I called the pet store to see if the puppies were still there. They were and I placed a hold on them. Oh no. Trouble.

Now, keep in mind that Randy has been watching me have an emotional meltdown at least once a week if not every few days for the previous four months. So if IG puppies were the answer then he was all in. The logistics of having four dogs was acknowledged but quickly dismissed as not a concern. Then we sprang the potential news to his mother who suggested Romeo and Juliet as names and then I was sold!

I went off to go look at the puppies with my dogs in tow to make sure everyone was going to get along. A few hours later I was walking to my car with the help of the pet store assistant with my puppies, my dogs, and puppy supplies. We loaded up my truck, I expressed my thanks, and got on the road. Halfway home I panicked: *Wait, WHAT HAVE I DONE?*

Here is something else to keep in mind. I was planning on having an estate sale in less than two weeks from this point. I had never had a garage sale let alone an estate sale. I would be selling my parents' worldly goods. Some items we had had in the house since I was born. I had so much stuff, in fact, people were telling me I couldn't possibly sell it all in a three-day sale and I would need to prepare to have another sale in a couple of weeks.

So what did I do? I bought puppies…not one but two…of a breed I was barely familiar with and had never really expressed an interest in owning. Ever. Distraction? Daydreaming? Craziness? Nope, not happening. Nothing to see here, folks; just move along.

By the end of the evening I had a backup plan. I remembered several years earlier my beloved Great-Aunt Helen had been in a convalescent home and was unable to keep her dog with her. This made me very sad and I knew it affected her quality of life. At the time I decided there should be a service that would help care for animals in this type of situation so their owners could benefit from the animals' companionship. So why not use these puppies as a pilot program. They could be therapy dogs that I either place in a home with these wraparound services to be provided or I could train them as therapy dogs and take them to convalescent homes since their size was easy to manage and they loved to be held. Problem solved.

Except for the fact that I had four dogs and it was less than a week before the estate sale in which I would sell my parents' worldly possessions and have a bunch of strangers in their once very guarded home…no problem!

I wasn't sleeping much those days so getting up to take care of the puppies gave me a purpose in the middle of the night. My youngest dog felt these were, in fact, her puppies and spent much of her waking hours caring for them. So life went on, the estate sale went well as previously discussed, and my longtime neighbor from across the street fell in love with the puppies.

Over the next two months, she would help watch them if I had to go out of town, and then she and her husband decided they would keep Romeo and Juliet. What life-savers they were and what a lesson on impulsive shopping! I couldn't have asked for a better home for the puppies and they were well suited to their new owners. I would take the dogs back should the neighbors not be able to care for them due to health reasons (I don't think this would be an issue but I'm happy to be the backup plan). So in a very backward way, it worked out but it was definitely an example of forcing something due to tunnel vision.

Now, why did I think this was a good distraction at the time? Because I was desperate. I was tired of feeling crappy; I wanted to feel better, feel like there was hope that I had something to look forward to. I love animals. They are healing to me, so why not have this great unplanned distraction that would give me a positive purpose?

Now it would have been a lot easier to deal with this logic if I had known it consciously, but once again hindsight is twenty-twenty, so this is what I learned from asking why. I don't think I could have answered anything other than I want them at the time and if someone had said give it twenty-four hours (and I listened to their advice), I probably wouldn't have gotten them. But I wouldn't have learned anything either. I would have still sought out external stimulus for an internal sadness.

I didn't have the typical grief reaction. I knew why I was in this situation. I was grateful I could take time to make this my focus in life and work to sort out all these loose ends. It was just a crappy situation and I was tired of feeling crappy. Do I regret it? No, because the dogs are in a great home and I learned a valuable lesson. I would be happy to care for them should it come to that in the future.

The bigger question for me was what was I supposed to do with my life once these loose ends were resolved. I felt I learned a lot about myself going through my separation and divorce. But I also realized I was in that relationship because I had forced it. What would have happened if I hadn't forced it? Would I have still learned these lessons; would my life have been any easier? While asking these questions I was also working on my relationship with God and reconnecting to a church body. I found great solace in going to church and feeling the love in the room. I also discovered a concept that was new to me: God's perfect will versus God's permissive will. When a person is really connected to God they can pray about concerns and work through issues using their prayer time and fellowship time to identify God's will for their life. God's perfect will allows for things to go smoothly and for opportunities to work themselves out without forcing. God's permissive will, on the other hand, gets a person through a situation they placed themselves in and now need to work through.

So have I lived my life in God's permissive will or perfect will? I would have to say permissive will and that bothers me. I am grateful for free will and I believe it allows the spiritual connection to be that much stronger when everything is in place, but it's got to be exhausting watching someone force situations their whole life and keep having to provide workable outs if they want to get through them. I want to live my life in God's perfect will, and that means I really need to become aware of when I want to force something.

This is a scary concept for me because as much as I say I believe in the Lord and he is my savior and I want him in charge, really letting go but being an active force in my own life is a fine balance and I'm a klutz!

My biggest downfall is I get impatient. I want to know what the plan is—what is the next step? So I come up with a plan and then I push to make it happen. It sounds logical, so why won't this work? Because I don't get the big picture. We were not created to get the big picture. Our instance to have knowledge and wisdom got us kicked out of the garden and we have been fighting ever since. Thank the Lord, He is forgiving because I look at my life and I feel like I can't say sorry enough…whoops my bad…again…ugh! It's so frustrating. And yet, isn't this what life is all about? Living life, making mistakes, hopefully learning from our mistakes only to make them again and get more knowledge.

Sure, but it's a lot easier said than done. I understand why people get overwhelmed, why they give up, why they just want relief from the pain. However, when we give in to our primal need for relief, we spin out of control and burden our lives with more lessons to learn.

CHAPTER 15

What Dreams Are Made Of...

My LIFE WAS A BLUR after my parents passed away. There was so much to do: planning their memorials both in the States and in Sweden, managing their estates and my own life. When I went to Sweden, it was a wonderful opportunity to hear their stories and to spend time with the people who had known my parents the longest.

It was during this trip I had my first zombie dream about my mother.

I'm not a fan of zombies—an odd statement, I know, but with all the zombie video games, movies, and television series, I feel the need to make this statement. So I was especially taken aback when my mother first appeared in a dream as a zombie.

I have had three dreams in the past of people close to me appearing to me before they passed. The first was my dear Aunt Helen. She was the matriarch of my father's family and came to live with my family while we lived in London for eight months. She walked me to and from school every day and we shopped at stores like Fortnum & Mason and Harrods, wandered the streets of London, visited the zoo, walked in Hyde Park and Windsor Castle, and rode the double-decker bus.

She was more than a Great Aunt; she was very dear to me.

We had a nightly ritual in London. She would turn on the radio while we were getting ready for bed, and once we were ready she would announce it was time to go to sleep and she would tuck me into bed with my favorite brown blanket covered with playful horses. My dream about Aunt Helen featured this same scene, except I, as an adult, looked on as the scene unfolded in front of me. This time, instead of announcing it was time for bed, she said, "It's time for me to go." I, as the adult, said "It's OK. I love you. Thank you for everything." She smiled and I looked at the clock radio and noted the time: five fifteen. I woke up. The next evening, I found out my Great-Aunt Helen had passed away just a few hours before at 5:15 p.m. Thank you, Aunt Helen, for coming to say goodbye. I love you.

Several years later, my husband's ailing grandmother came to me in a dream. My now ex-husband and I had met while he was living with his grandmother in Riverside, California. She, too, was the matriarch of the family, and he had gone there to get his act together (I found this out later). She was a strong, spiritual woman and I enjoyed our visits. I knew her for several years before her health declined. At this point, she had moved to Northern California to be close to my ex's family. She had hospice and family caring for her. I dreamed about her visiting me at the edge of our bed while I was sleeping. She was at the foot of the bed, standing with her right arm extended out onto the footrest to steady herself, and she was on my side. My ex remained asleep, unaware she was there. I asked her, "What do you need?" She said, "I'm tired and I want to go." I said, "It's OK. You can go. You have done all you can do." Her bright blue eyes gleamed and I went back to sleep. Apparently, the next day she woke up and asked my mother-in-law, who was at her bedside, "Am I still alive?" She and the few others in the room giggled fondly and said, "Yes, you are still with us." She had good visits with all of her family that week and died a week after the night of my dream.

The third dream was about my Swedish grandmother, my mother's mother, Gerd. Gerd loved to sit outside in the sun with her husband. Whenever we visited them or they visited us, they always made a point of spending some time sitting in the sun. Gerd came to me in my dream while I was leaving work to go on my lunch break. She said, "Let's eat at an outdoor café. You need to make a point of spending thirty minutes in the sun every day. You need to take time to slow down and relax." I said, "This is good advice. I need to listen to this." She said, "Yes, you do," with a stern but smiling face. We spent time chatting and relaxing under a warm, reassuring sun. The next day, my father called to tell me she had passed away. I told him about my dream and he was surprised but happy to hear about it.

So, you can imagine, after all this I wondered whether my parents would come to me before they passed, and if they did, what would they say? They didn't, much to my disappointment.

Instead, while winding down on the last days of my trip in Sweden I experienced my first zombie dream about my mother. Since my mother's passing, I'd had a hard time picturing her at peace. She had rarely been at peace while she was alive. She had expressed to me on several occasions a desire to be at peace mentally but was unable to find a way to make that happen.

My first dream was set in the old downtown area of my hometown. My mother was wandering the area, slightly disheveled, looking for something. She met up with her oldest friend (who lives in Sweden, but thankfully these kinds of details are always nonissues in dreams) and together they found me at my parents' house. We met on the back patio, where my mother's friend, with my mother in tow, asked me if I could help find my mother some clothes. She was tired and dirty and wanted to freshen up. I panicked! Her clothes! They had been sorted, all of her closets had been moved around, and, most importantly, her underwear had been thrown away. What was I going to do? How was I going to fix this? She would be furious with me once she discovered what had happened. Then I woke up, anxious but relieved to be awake. I told my boyfriend about my dream and he tried to console me, but it stayed with me all that day as we toured old town Stockholm. That night I dreamed she was back to wandering the streets of my hometown. This time, the police were involved and they had sought me out to help corral my mother, since she had escaped the morgue and needed to be put down. When we found her she was disheveled and disoriented, not herself, and she went with the police peacefully.

Since then I have had a few more dreams more along the nature of the first rather than the second. The dreams always come during high-stress times and leave me longing for the ability to have my mother at rest in my own mind. I created a plan to help facilitate this process. Once everything settled down I would spend some time in the South of France, a place she had spent her childhood summers and always spoke wistfully about when she chose to reminisce.

It had been eighteen months since my parents had passed, the estate was nearly settled, and the few items left could be managed by phone. I chose to change venues and moved to the inner northwest (northwest Idaho). At the time of this decision but before the move, my boyfriend and I started watching the television show *The Walking Dead*. After the second night, I had another zombie dream about my mother. This time, when I came across her, I shouted, "Be at peace!" and forced a piece of rebar through her chest. I'm well aware of the fact that this is a violent and completely disturbing image. However, so is being haunted by the zombie version of your mother…a walking corpse that resembles someone you know and love and yet you know it is not them because their soul is gone. I guess it took a few hours of watching people face their loved ones and strangers in zombie form to realize the importance of destroying the form to preserve the person, their soul. Despite the gory scene I previously described with my mother, I felt and she looked at peace for the first time in years…literally!

I was glad I had watched the show and continued to do so throughout our move and once there as we set up our new home. After the first few hectic days of sorting out rooms, furniture, and boxes, the house started to come together and I began to relax. I had another dream about my mother—the best one yet.

I was driving her old car (a red convertible Mercedes Benz 500 SL). I had just parked in the parking structure of an affluent mall in Orange County. I was getting my dog out of the backseat and placing her plush harness and leash on. We were getting ready to meet my mother for lunch. It was her birthday. I arrived early, as I am prone to do, to meet with the host of the restaurant (a high-end French restaurant, where ladies lunch) to review the details of the afternoon. There were several women in the plush waiting area, where I was speaking with the host, when my mother arrived. He recognized her first—my mother had a regal demeanor and people always recognized her—so it was no surprise to me that he noticed her and said to me, "There she is. Let's welcome her with a song."

Everyone started singing "Happy Birthday." My mother, not realizing the song was for her, continued down the walkway looking for me. I had to scurry to catch up to her and get her attention. "Mom, the song is for you. Happy birthday!" She stopped, realized that it was for her, and smiled at all her friends. She looked amazing. She was dressed in a thick raw-silk, cross-weave-bodice, tea-length white strapless gown. It showed off all of her best features and she was happy. We sat together, opposite one another, and chatted the lunch away. She taught me phrases in French and was happy with my pronunciation. We were happy together. After lunch, I had arranged for us to relax in the neighboring solarium. I was awakened by the host, who was now the young mortician who had come to pick up my mother's body the night she had passed away. He said, in a very kind gentle manner, "Helena, your mother is gone. She passed away in her sleep. She is at peace." I got up from my chair and saw that she was at peace and then woke from the dream. I had finally experienced the relationship with my mother I had always wanted and now I could be a peace with her. Thank you, Mom.

CHAPTER 16

The Key to Understanding My Mother Is Provence

FEELING SUPPORTED THROUGH TOUGH TIMES is critical to getting through the struggle without additional injury. I know this is true both professionally and personally and yet I still struggle to ask for help. I don't want to burden anyone. My mother was very big on manners. Good manners dictate that you not be a burden to anyone, only a pleasure to be around. She wanted to ensure that I did the family proud, so I was taught table manners and proper protocol around adults, other children, and strangers. You name the situation and my mother had a protocol for it. It boiled down to staying quiet and out of the way, not drawing attention to yourself. Unless someone looks like they need help or asks you for help, you leave people to themselves.

This was how my mother had been raised. My maternal grandmother was half-French and half-Swedish. Both cultures revolve around hospitality and manners. I discovered this again when I went on a trip to Provence, France, and Sweden by myself in May of 2013.

Both cultures take great pride in hospitality. The French want people to appreciate their history and their country's riches, both in production of goods and in scenery. Each region of France has a specialty, producing amazing things that range from goat cheese to lavender to beautiful locally spun linens to rare spices like saffron. And, of course, each region in France is known for its particular wine, and the list goes on. Everywhere you go in France, especially southern France, there is a cornucopia of choices of local fare. If you are not wowed by this, then the locals feel they have not honored their country correctly. The other option is that you are an idiot to not appreciate all they have to offer. Americans have unfortunately gained the idiot status. This is because Americans tend to be over the top in responses, making too big of a deal about something, drawing too much attention, which makes their host uncomfortable, or not allowing an experience to linger but moving on to the next thing too quickly without understanding the complexity of the item they just sampled or purchased. The French have their own timing. To be out of step with the timing draws attention to yourself. This is very un-French.

If you allow yourself to be wowed by the French culture and take time to be quiet and enjoy their way of living then you will be welcomed. This welcome is understated. It means you are accepted as a part of the scenery versus taking away from the scenery. The point in France is to blend in, but to blend in means to be French. If you are not French, then you need to appreciate everything that is French: speak French if you know it, do not create a French accent (if you did not earn it, it is not yours to mimic—it is perceived as a mockery versus trying to fit in), and wear similar clothing (stylish and simple, not flashy). If you don't know what something is, ask, but don't expect a long answer. If you want a history lesson you take a tour or look it up. In other words, channel your inner French. If you are not interested then don't complain when they are rude to you, because that will be the result.

In Sweden, on the other hand, the hospitality is all about feeling comfortable. The public spaces are clean, the locals are friendly and welcoming, and the stores gift wrap your packages as normal fare. The food is comfort food: meatballs and potatoes. It is easy to be comfortable in Sweden. Swedes learn to speak English early on in school and love the opportunity to practice. So it is easy to travel within the country if you don't speak the language. Swedes love Americans; they are happy to be entertained by our perceived loudness and lack of understanding of how things work. Their tolerance of our differences makes visiting Sweden very easy.

My mother was very French. She loved her French side of the family and spoke of them in a wistful manner. The time she had spent with them as a child informed her way of being and perceiving the world. To her, everyone should behave as the French do, culturally speaking, not politically or bureaucratically. We should be considerate of others: blend in, do not draw attention to yourself, respect the culture you are in, learn the language, and understand the history. Respect the history.

Deviating from this meant you were not only disrespecting the family, you were disrespecting my mother. People whom my mother deemed disrespectful were then labeled idiots. Idiots never got a second chance. Redemption was found in neutrality. The hope was that they would begin to blend in and stop acting like idiots by disobeying the above "rules."

I don't think my mother ever labeled me an idiot, but I know she spent most of her life unhappy with my choices. I was a person she never understood or could relate to and had she not been present for my birth, she probably would have thought that the stork had dropped me off. I spent the majority of my life trying to live up to her expectations and her rules.

Over the years I learned the importance of social support systems and how invaluable the feeling of being supported can be despite the rule that we do not seek outside support lest we disrespect the family. I still struggle to ask for support. I happily support others but rarely allowed them to return the favor since I might burden them and thereby shame my family.

I struggled with this conscious/unconscious message for years and started to break through it while contemplating divorce. When I went through the divorce I felt the invaluable support, and once through my nightmare, I knew I could get through anything as long as I used my close friends as support. I nicknamed them "the dream team."

While my parents were sick it was easy to reach out. Each memorial was an opportunity to build on this support. Since my mother had always been so concerned about my potential burden on others I didn't spend a lot of time with either family without my parents' supervision, if you will. In 2008, I broke tradition and went to Sweden on my own to establish my own relationship with my family there and to spend time with my ailing grandmother. I did this several years in a row much to my mother's chagrin.

I also made a point to visit family on my father's side for the same reason. This made spending time with all of them during the difficult time of my parents' passing much easier. And in the subsequent months we built stronger relationships so that now I truly feel blessed by their support and I am confident I am not shaming my parents.

Dream Team Becomes a Community Thing...

The week before the first estate sale, I was knee-deep in self-imposed puppy distraction, prepping for the sale by organizing the various rooms, garage spaces, and patios, and Randy was not feeling well. Five days before the sale, he had gone to the emergency room at the Long Beach VA only to be admitted for pancreatitis due to an inflamed gallbladder that needed to be removed once his pancreas settled down. Did I mention that my father died of pancreatic cancer? Are you kidding me? Randy, my boyfriend was in the hospital with an inflamed pancreas five days before the estate sale, when I would open my family home up to the community for the first time ever. Ever! I was horrified on many levels. I called in the support team and I told Randy's family that I needed them to visit him because I had to get through the sale. Of course, I felt like an ass.

Randy felt terrible, of course, both physically and emotionally. The irony of the situation did not escape him. He was trapped in the hospital. He felt terrible because of the timing, he understood I needed to stay at the house and prepare. He also knew that if he took a turn for the worse I would be there and if need be I would cancel the sale. As it turned out, he stabilized while in the hospital and wanted to be released in time for the sale. I asked him to stay in since I didn't want to worry about him and the sale. He begrudgingly agreed.

The day before the sale a member of the dream team called me to see how I was doing. Was I ready, did I need anything before she came over to help, was I concerned about the weather because the weather forecast was rain? "No, no, I'm not concerned. It won't rain. The weather forecasters are always wrong." Famous last words.

On the morning of the first day, under threatening skies, we had a line of people waiting to get into the sale. All of my volunteers had arrived. This included family friends of both my parents, our housekeeper from when I was a child, the neighbors across the street, Randy's family, and some of his friends. It was a family affair. We had coffee, tea, and breakfast treats. Everyone had their assigned stations, price points, and negotiation ranges. We were ready, and then it started to rain.

After an hour of steady light rain I finally agreed we needed to cover all the outside sale items with clear, light plastic sheets. A friend rushed out to get it and after another hour everything was covered. That's when it started to pour! We were standing in an inch of water in some places. But that didn't stop the sale; people just kept on coming.

It was a three-day sale and during this time I discovered my family was bonding with the customers. People learned the story of my family: my mother's sophisticated taste, my father's crafty hobbies like furniture assembly, his vast tool collection, and my parents' book collections. Customers came back several times each day bringing with them their own friends and family to partake in the sale and hear the stories. It was a community affair.

My cavalier approach to opening my family home to sell many beautiful things allowed the local community to share in our culture and our lives. It became an event for their families to share in the experience. Our shared experience and joy in each item was very French...

TRANSITIONS

The second estate sale was smaller and held by a team of professionals while I helped host a fundraiser in Los Angeles for an organization supporting eating disorder recovery. By the end of the second sale 70 percent of the stuff had been sold and I donated the rest that I was not keeping. As a thank you to my family and friends I held a Christmas tea open house. I knew it would be my last Christmas in the house and I wanted friends and family to enjoy it.

In January of 2012, I worked with more friends, who also happened to own a great contracting company, to get the house ready to be sold. In addition to prepping my family home for sale, I started planning my fortieth birthday celebration. Each day up until to my birthday weekend was filled with the many details that come with saying goodbye to the small things and letting go of a family home. I had a great birthday weekend with family and friends at the end of March. I placed the house on the real estate market after my birthday celebration. It was a tough day when the "For Sale" sign went up in the front yard.

During my birthday weekend, I met a veterinarian who was a teacher at a local vet school. I told him about my previous interest in veterinary medicine and he encouraged me to look into it again. He offered to give me a tour of the school and I accepted.

I wanted a change. I was in a unique position. I could return to my old life as a program director for a residential treatment program, I could go into private practice full time, or I could do something else. I decided to explore vet school.

I spent the summer preparing my applications, starting a volunteer position at a small animal hospital, and preparing to go back to school, at the ripe age of forty, since I needed a couple of prerequisites. I took ecology, genetics, and biochemistry. Each class had a lab, so now, twenty years after my last undergraduate class, I found myself in a classroom again. I was old enough to be these students' mother and I felt it. I did reasonably well in my classes despite a rough start and I learned a great deal at the small animal hospital.

I spent Christmas 2012 in an intentionally quiet way, away from everyone. Randy, the dogs, and I relaxed in a mountain cabin, where, for the first time in two years, I started to relax, really relax. I started to rethink vet school, but I wanted to wait to see if I got into any of the schools before I made any final decisions.

I got accepted to the University of Glasgow, Scotland, and faced my decision. Do I change my career, add to it, or just stick with what I know. I love Scotland. I think the Scottish Highlands is the most magical place on Earth. So moving to Scotland for five years sounded fabulous. But I decided I enjoyed working as a therapist too much to change careers and adding to a career is not realistic at my age. I was happy I went through the process of torturing my brain back into learning and growing. I will never regret not going to vet school. I know I'm happy with what I do for a living. I did realize I wanted to change something. It was time to move.

Since the estate organizing was coming to a close, my school adventures were completed, and I had a plan forming for the future, I decided it was time for a trip to the South of France to connect to the things my mother loved—perhaps to understand her better. Once again, friends helped me plan my trip.

They directed me to a walking tour company. I soon found out this was the best way to go. The first part of my trip was a walking tour of Provence, France. Then I visited family friends in the west of France for a few days and, finally, spent the last two weeks in Sweden to visit with family.

As it turns out, I found peace with my mother through my dreams before my trip. But I had already bought the tickets for the trip and made plans with family so I decided to go anyway. Sometimes life really gives you tough choices…

It was a tremendous trip, better than I could have predicted. Each day in Provence reminded me of my mother: all the white linen clothing stores my mother would have regularly patronized (I probably had enough white linen to open my own store prior to the estate sales), the décor of the old Roman village bed and breakfast (my mother had the same style of chairs and sofas), not to mention an old travel poster of a woman who could have been my mother in her early twenties. The exact same throw pillow in my parents' library was in a random restaurant we chose to eat lunch in one day! The examples continue, but I think you get the point. Everywhere I looked, my mother's presence and taste were felt and it was reassuring to see her.

The rest of the trip was cathartic. It was the first time I had seen my family since the memorial in Sweden almost two years before. We spent our time reminiscing about my parents and my family and creating new memories.

RESPECT

I use the term *family* for people whom I'm related to by blood as well as people who have been in my life from the beginning. My mother's oldest friend is family. She and I went to lunch my last day in Sweden. My mother and her friend were known for their style and fashionable taste in their college years and this never changed. Both had exquisite taste in their homes. Their personas and their lives reflected it in everything they did.

We went to Burger King for lunch. This is not odd even though it seems to contradict what I just shared because I spent every visit I've ever had with her having one meal at a McDonald's for a connection to my American roots. We couldn't find a McDonald's so Burger King was the next best thing.

As we got out of the car she apologized for her sloppy look. She wore a classic navy pleated trouser, a white blouse, and brown belt with coordinated loafers. She decided to pull the look together with a scarf she had in the back of her car. I said, "You know we are going into Burger King. I don't think anyone is going to think you are underdressed." Her response will stay with me for the rest of my life.

"Helena, I am not doing this for them. I am dressing out of respect for you."

I was speechless. So many things came together for me in an instant.

My mother dressed out of respect to who she was seeing and what she was doing. She expected the same of others, especially me. Her frustration with my "jeans and T-shirt uniform" was seen as disrespectful to her or anyone I was around unless I was working in the yard or riding a horse.

This all came rushing at me as the profoundness of her statement hit me: "I am dressing out of respect for you."

Think about how much our culture has changed with regard to how we dress. Now it is commonplace to see people in workout clothes running errands, wearing jeans in nice restaurants, and wearing pajamas when they travel.

We have lost a sense of respect in how we approach people or how they perceive us. This "take me as I am" attitude has become an in-your-face uniform.

What a different place our world might be if we made an effort to respect one another: a just-pulled-together outfit for a simple lunch with the ones we love and respect.

CHAPTER 17

Be Careful What You Wish For...

LIFE IN IDAHO.

Despite the fact that some people in my circle viewed the move to Idaho as spontaneous, I had done my research. I moved to Idaho because I still wanted to be on the west side of the country. I didn't want to be on the coast because I had thankfully had that experience for most of my life. I did want to be near water. I wanted to be near a city but with open space, fewer people. On a previous road trip in 2012, Randy and I had stopped in Coeur d'Alene, Idaho, to visit a friend. So when it was time to move, I knew where I wanted to go.

I spent the next few months before to the move researching what the mental health community was like, what the needs were, and who was doing the work. When I returned from my trip to France and Sweden, it was time to meet the programs I had learned about during my research. The first place I went to check out was the stables. I ended up working for them for the next two years.

THE STABLES

Randy and I went out to the stables to see the facilities, to learn about their program, and to introduce ourselves. In the first meeting, I discovered from one of the owners of the facility that the stables had been working with a local nonprofit developing a partnership to provide a "ranch experience" for at-risk youth. Since I had a background in working with addictions, developing programs, and creating experiential programs, specifically equine therapy, it seemed like the perfect fit. I discovered a month later how fortuitous this would be. In the fall of 2012, while I was in school and applying for veterinary school, the stables and the nonprofit partnership were creating a job description that appeared to read directly from my résumé.

Over the years, I have discovered most programs meant to care for others also find themselves burdened by their own needs. When creating a program, the purpose needs to be clear, without the distraction of internal conflict. My timing at the stables allowed the program creators the opportunity to identify what they wanted their purpose to be in the community. I helped them develop a multifaceted program.

This opportunity allowed me to learn the culture of the area. Outside of the stables, I became the networking coordinator for the model of equine therapy I was trained in and learned all the different programs offering any kind of equine-related work and who they were offering the work to, what population did they seek to help? I believe we all grow from strategic partnerships and can support one another. Sometimes the support ends up encouraging people to go in different directions. My hope was to build my business by creating multiple contracts with organizations like the stables. But instead, I helped them determine that their direction did not include me or my company in the long term.

I was taken in by the dream that while I was sweating over what to do with my life someone was out there creating my dream job. It was a beautiful thought but not the reality.

This opportunity allowed me to gain clarity on what I want for myself both professionally and personally. Part of me was tired of trying to figure stuff out. I just wanted to go to work, take care of my horses, and live my life. Instead, I found myself personally and professionally challenged.

I have discovered I thrive when challenged. It gives me clarity on what I believe in and what I believe is important. I discovered the best alliances are the ones that fit naturally; we work well together and thrive under pressure. Partnerships that fracture under pressure are ones that will not last.

REDEMPTION

A few months after settling into life in Coeur d'Alene, I was entertaining myself by horse shopping on the Internet. I came across an ad from a local horse breeder who only bred a few horses a year and also had a photography studio, so all their ads were beautifully done. I came across this beautiful blue gray filly walking in the tall grass. Her name was Redemption because she had been born on Easter morning. She was a Percheron quarter-horse cross, a combination I had wanted since high school, and she was a blue roan, my favorite horse color. I called just for fun. There was no way she was still available.

Redemption was still available. Hallelujah!

It took several more weeks for me to get out to meet her, so I was convinced she would be sold, but she was still there, waiting. My blue roan Percheron quarter-horse cross was waiting for me. She greeted me in the pasture with curiosity and willingness. We negotiated a deal on the spot and I came back a week later to pick her up. She loaded into the trailer without any issue, rode to her new home quietly, and settled into her new space without incident. I brought her to the stables on the anniversary of my parents' wedding. They would have been married for forty-nine years.

This filly has been so easy to teach. Her willingness to gain new skills, security in life, and general contentment is inspirational to all who are around her. I have Redemption in my life and share her willingly. Her barn name is Arya, named after a book character who is mighty despite the trials in her life.

DAKOTA

Four months later, just before Christmas 2013, I got an email from a website I forgot existed. The website's name was dreamhorse.com. I was notified that there was a 100 percent match for my dream dressage show horse: a bay Lusitano gelding proven at Prix St. George and trained almost through Grand Prix. Lusitanos are a baroque horse, a group of horses originally bred to train in dressage. This dream horse list was topped by the fact that the horse's name was Talento and he was imported from Spain. He was the real deal and there was definitely no way he was still available. No way. I called for fun.

He was still available, and despite the fact that I wasn't completely settled in my life, meaning I didn't own a house and the job thing was unsteady, I arranged to go see him, back in Southern California. I found him to be amazing but decided I should be an adult. It was premature to invest my money in this venture so I reluctantly accepted this choice and promptly pouted for a good thirty minutes. Then I got a call from a friend.

She said a mutual friend was looking to sell their draft mare that they hadn't owned long. She was originally from North Dakota and lived in Southern California with a person who had struggled with addiction and could no longer keep her. They were no longer able to care for her and the horse went to our mutual friends who brushed up her skills and helped her find a home. Since I was passing on Talento and still in Southern California, I went to see her. I liked her immediately and found her fun to ride. Yep, I bought a horse on that trip, just not the one I had gone to visit originally.

She arrived a month later on a snowy cold day in northern Idaho. She considered not getting out of the trailer when she took a look at all the white stuff on the ground and got a whiff of the cold air but then obediently came out. She settled into a routine once she survived her first night of being visited by elk and moose—poor thing was shaking despite the three layers of blankets. It was then I realized not all the footprints in the snow were horse. Her name was Dakota and I decided she needed a new name to complete her fresh start. I called her Luna after her light and dark colors, after much waxing and waning after my new beginnings.

CHAPTER 18

The Best Is Yet To Come

I MOURN THE LOSS OF my parents every day. But in the first few years, each month had its own meaning. The first year I learned the pattern of pain that would be around for the next few years of my life.

TIME TRAVEL

June: no explanation needed. July: I received their ashes, my father's memorial, and my parents' memorial in Sweden. Fourth of July was always special to me growing up. My dad made a point of being home to celebrate; he cooked hamburgers on the grill. My mother always talked about the Founding Fathers and the Declaration of Independence, its history and signing. August: I dispersed my parents' ashes on the day of their wedding anniversary. In 2011, they would have been married for forty-seven years.

September 5 was my mother's birthday. October 4 was my father's birthday. November: We had almost always spent Thanksgiving together regardless of other dramas in our lives. December: Christmas. We celebrated Christmas Eve, a Swedish tradition. My mother always rallied for Christmas. She cooked one of three Swedish dishes she had learned from her mother, set a beautiful table, and decorated the living room. Her last Christmas was at home. My father and I cooked the meal. I set the table and we decorated the living room. Mom was there with more energy and engagement than she had been in the previous few months. It was the last time I saw a true glimmer of my mother.

January is easiest month because I have survived the holidays. But now thinking back to my mother's passing, in January she took a turn for the worse and I knew she would not survive the year. My father was becoming tired and not feeling well but was not sure why. February: My father always celebrated Valentine's Day with my mother and myself. He gave us cards, flowers, chocolates, or all three. He always remembered this holiday, even in his last year. March is when I celebrate my birthday. Our family tradition was to bring a breakfast tray to the birthday person's bed. Birthdays were always special to my mother and therefore to our family. My last birthday with them was spent with both of my parents. My mother was home after having spent three months in various hospital settings. She was a shell of herself and barely present. My father was exhausted and beyond overwhelmed. But still they both smiled when he offered me flowers from their garden and wished me happy birthday. I was thirty-nine and heartbroken.

April was the calm before the storm. In May the hammer was dropped and life as I knew it was almost over.

The second year after my parents' passing was painful but there were not as many tears. The third year was the worst. I couldn't remember them as clearly. The pain that was so consistent was starting to wane and I was realizing on a whole new level that my parents were gone and I was on my own.

The fourth year was so much better than the previous years but I didn't realize I was still frozen, just in a new way: a slow-moving glacier.

MEMORIES

I made a photo collage of my parents and my family home before I left California. I set my dad's to "It Was a Very Good Year" by Frank Sinatra and my mother's to "That's Life" by Frank Sinatra. So when I found myself crying three years after their passing to the song "The Best Is Yet to Come" by Blue Eyes himself. I know it's a sign.

"It Was a Very Good Year": I chose the song for my dad's slide show because I felt this song was about a man's progression of awareness through his life. My father was reflective, perhaps not always aware but he was introspective. The shift and changes that occurred during his life are highlighted by eras, such as the amazing experiences as a child growing up in Africa, as a teenager in central California with the beginnings of the American hot rod and its surrounding culture, his twenties as a student of life, then at thirty-four completed medical school with a young family and living as a doctor carving out the life he would lead, doing all of the wonderful hobbies that gave him such joy. In his last days he had been looking back on his life; I don't think he had any real regrets. He had a good life; it was a very good year, a very good life. He was at peace.

"That's Life" was my mother's song.

My mother lived a very pragmatic life. Early on she did many different things; she "fell down" quite a bit but it never seemed to discourage her or stop her. She was determined to have it her way. She was determined to live life and to take it on her terms. There were a few times she became very discouraged and thought about being done with life but never succumbed to those thoughts. She would ultimately not allow it to happen until finally, at the end, when her body really had given up on her and her soul mate had a fatal condition. Only then was it time. On her terms, she decided to let go of her mortal coil and embrace her spirit. "That's Life" is emblematic of her charismatic spirit, how she lived her life, and how she left it.

It's A Sign

It was July 2014. We had family in town and it was Fourth of July. I wanted to rally to honor the past and my family. The reality of true loss was hitting me on levels I didn't think were possible. I was overwhelmed by everything. My work was tumultuous as contracts were in flux. I was in the process of buying a home, and getting a mortgage approved took an act of Congress; it was a totally intrusive process to one's personal and professional life. I was questioning every decision I'd ever made and just wanted to go hide in a hole.

Somehow the slow-moving glacier called Helena got through the visit without offending anyone and we were sending the last of the family home with lunch out at a nice restaurant prior to taking them to the airport. It was a lovely lunch and time to go. I ran to the restroom. The restroom audio was playing jazz/blues.

Then I heard it: "The Best Is Yet to Come."

"The Best Is Yet to Come" is obviously about a new romantic relationship, but I had a different take on it when I heard it.

My parents always seemed liked these formidable forces I was trying to keep up with in my childhood and young adult life. It was a struggle for me to even compare let alone honor them in what I thought they wanted me to become in life. I'd worked hard to honor their memories physically, emotionally, and spiritually. I found myself trying to carve out a new life, moving on with their memories but not their physical presence. In hearing the song "The Best Is Yet to Come" I heard them speaking to me about successes that were near or things I hoped would come together.

The best is yet to come…they were part of me now in a different way; they would help me create a new life for myself, backing me in my successes, clearing the way for new opportunities. If I did my due diligence then I would succeed; whether it was with the house, the business, even the horses, I felt my parents were helping me grow, to be better than I could ever be, maybe even with them here.

Despite my previous statement of utter sadness at the loss of my parents, I am truly grateful for so many things. I could be there for them when the time had come. I inherited their lives (the good, bad, and ugly), which afforded me the opportunity to change my life, move away, and start over. I was buying a house with property; I had beautiful horses, wonderful support, a loving partner. Life was good.

Hearing the song in the stall of this bathroom "The Best Is Yet to Come," I knew they were still looking out for me. I realized that even though my parents were gone from this world, I was not alone. They were watching over me. They were looking out for me, and somehow it was going to be OK, more than OK. Not only were they watching out for me, but I was not forsaken. My father would take care of me, and my parents would help me in ways I couldn't foresee.

Now I was sobbing—thankfully not the ugly cry you can't hide because your face is a different color and the snot and tears are too copious to manage, but a deep cry. After a few minutes, I recovered enough to pull myself together to take our family to the airport.

The glacier had melted to a thick sludge.

Grace Manor

A month later my mortgage was approved. On the same day, I turned in the keys to the rental, our home for the past two years, and I received the keys to my new home. It was on a ridge line, a few minutes outside of town, just shy of ten acres with an apartment over a garage to rent. There was a lovely family already renting and who had agreed to stay. There was space for horses, eventually, although I was not ready for them yet. The property came with a name, etched in iron as you entered the drive: Grace Manor.

Our first year at Grace Manor was spent taking care of projects that had been neglected and getting it ready to bring horses on the property. We started having guests ten days after we moved in. Our guests helped with the property and the house. Grace Manor has become a place of rest and comfort for all, a place of peace as my family home was intended to be.

Obi-Wan Kenobi

The other thing that happened in July of 2014 was something I never thought would happen. The person who owned Talento, my dream horse, contacted me. She wanted to know if I was still interested in him. Yay, of course, but now I really couldn't afford him given the house and all the projects I was looking at taking on when we moved in. But I made an offer, just for fun, expecting her to say thanks but no thanks, especially since I couldn't pay the final amount until September.

She took the offer. And much to my surprise, my dream horse was scheduled to arrive in October. When he arrived, I was out of town on a business trip and met him a few days later. The first day I rode him, he took three steps, stopped, turned around, and looked at me. I said "I know, buddy, I have a lot to learn/remember. I hope you will be patient with me." He continued but reluctantly. This became our dynamic and it is why I call him Obi for Obi-Wan Kenobi—because he is my dressage Jedi master and I am his Padawan.

Blue Moon Mending

I mentioned before I was building a business once I moved to Idaho. The focus of my business is to provide equine psychotherapy using the EAGALA (equine-assisted psychotherapy and equine-assisted learning) model and workshops and retreats for professionals in the mental health industry, and my client population focus is veterans and their families.

My company's name is Blue Moon Mending—where healing is never a rare event. The logo is inspired by Arya (Redemption), and the website is filled with images of both the girls, Luna and Arya, doing their thing. I started a blog intended to challenge thought and inspire internal musing. The first few years of building a business is about establishing who you are and what you have to offer. I have three locations to operate out of including Grace Manor. I have many ideas and hopes for the business. Time will tell if it succeeds.

Bright Heart Health

This company came to me right at a pivotal time when I really needed a regular paycheck. It is the first truly online, live-chat, telemedicine company. It is nationally recognized by important powers that be (JACHO—the Joint Commission on Accreditation of Healthcare Organizations) and it has tremendous potential. I love the team of people I work with; it is exciting to be a part of something from the start without it all being up to me to make it work. It is the wave of the future: accessibility for people with debilitating mental conditions or crazy work schedules or personal lives can now access top-quality care from the comfort of their own home. I'm excited to see where this company will grow and how I might grow with it.

CHAPTER 19

Politics-It's a family affair

"And now for something completely different…"

—MONTY PYTHON'S FLYING CIRCUS

MY MOTHER WAS A POLITICAL sponge. She loved debates, forming new ideas, defending old ideas/foundations for the political structure, and everything in between. As I mentioned before, she was an intellectual powerhouse, so debating my mother on politics, foreign or domestic, was a bold endeavor. She loved to listen to/read commentators like William F. Buckley, Rush Limbaugh, Sean Hannity, and journals like the *Atlantic*, the *Weekly Standard*, and the *Jerusalem Post*. This doesn't even touch the tip of the iceberg in the collection of books, newspaper clippings, and magazines my parents collected (mainly my mother). It's safe to say I grew up talking politics and I have a decent understanding of our political history and current environment.

I love my family. We are made up of very interesting characters. I have nine cousins: seven in the United States and two in Sweden. On the American side, we all get along, but, like any family, some of us resonate better with one another than others do. My grandfather was an inspiration to his children and their children. We all have our causes that we champion. We are all strongly opinionated and focused on our plans. However, we rarely speak about politics at our gatherings. In the past, when someone was bold enough to take on the topic, it was a sure thing you would hear my mother become animated, fired up, or, at some point, just rude. She was so frustrated by anyone who was not educated on politics. To her—and I agree with her premise, just not her execution—not understanding our politics is dismissing our hard-won freedom of speech, liberty, and the pursuit of happiness. It was an affront to our forefathers.

My Family Makes the Conservative News…

Each of us has events in our lives that are pivotal, moments you will remember forever because of your reaction to the event and knowledge/familiarity to the circumstance. The events of 9/11 is an example. We know where we were, what we were doing, and even what we were thinking at the time the news first hit us.

On a much smaller scale than 9/11, I remember the day my family made conservative news. Randy and I were on a road trip to visit a friend in north Idaho, a year before we moved up, and Ted Cruz was reading *Green Eggs and Ham* to the Senate. I remember feeling shocked and proud. I was curious where this would lead because I knew my family had plans.

Heidi Cruz is one of my first cousins. She is the only daughter of my father's sister. My Aunt Suzanne and Uncle Pete have spent their lives giving back to others in the form of missionary work both at home and abroad. They are an active family, which includes traveling to incredible places and doing amazing things. (This is true for the entire Rouhe clan). Heidi has one brother. He is an orthopedic surgeon. He and his family have been involved in missionary work for years in both the Dominican Republic and Haiti. He was first on the scene after the Haitian earthquake and spent ninety hours in surgery.

There are so many stories like this when it comes to my family it amazes me. I would go on but their stories are not mine to tell. I mention this background only to say that even for this crew having someone run for president of the United States of America is a big deal.

Heidi is married to Ted Cruz, the freshman senator from Texas who is running for president. Even as I write this he is in the top five of candidates for the Republican Party nomination for 2016.

Are You Kidding Me!!
My first cousin has a serious chance at becoming the first lady. WHAT?

Rush Limbaugh

The first time, I heard radio commentators comment on the wunderkind Ted Cruz I practically ran off the road. That's Heidi's husband! I went to their wedding. What is happening here? Rush Limbaugh was practically salivating all over his microphone, he was so excited to talk to Ted. This was long before Ted announced he was running for president (it was just a twinkle in his eye). Rush was talking to Ted about the work he was doing in the Senate and his determination to stand up for the Constitution. My mother would have been proud that someone else in the family was standing up for our forefathers!

Heidi and Ted created this plan a long time ago. When she first told me about their ambition I was supportive. But I honestly couldn't wrap my head around the idea. Heidi as the first lady. OK. I guess I say good luck? And try not to sound dismissive or snarky.

When Ted ran for the Senate position in Texas, I watched from afar with curiosity but I was skeptical. After all, he had not held public office, and, although his legal career was impressive, was it really enough? When he won I was amazed. They did it! Right on, good for them. My mother would have been tremendously impressed. She enjoyed watching his rise in politics in Texas, but unfortunately never got to see him win the Senate seat. I became more focused on my parents' stuff after the Senate win, so I stopped following his career for a while.

Then in 2013, we took our road trip to look for rentals in Coeur d'Alene and Ted was again in the news, becoming a fixture of the conservative Tea Party and creating his platform on health care, tax reform, and immigration. I was reminded that my family is a force to be reckoned with and I decided I'd better start paying attention to his career again.

Now I have more time to focus on politics and world events. It seems Ted is mentioned on a regular basis on conservative news on all fronts—radio, TV, and print.

March 2015. I was at the EAGALA conference. Blue Moon Mending was a sponsor for the event, I had several presentations during the conference, and we were hosting a lounge to encourage rest and reflection for conference participants. Plus I'm an EAGALA board member and I had responsibilities to the conference from the organization standpoint. I had my hands full.

I walked by a newsstand and saw Ted had announced he was running for president.

I stopped in the middle of a conversation, in the middle of a group of people, and walked over to the newsstand. "Are you OK?" came from several people at one time. Yay—that's my cousin.

"What? Ted Cruz? Are you kidding me?"

Now, the announcement wasn't a huge surprise to me. I knew from my conversations with family that Heidi and Ted were seriously considering this decision. But the timing, announcing so early, I knew they had their reasons. It has been fascinating to watch how they have played out their long-term game plan.

As I write this, Ted is in the top five of the candidate field. He is strategically placing himself to stay in the pack, standing firm on what he believes in and eloquently speaking his concerns.

Regardless of people's political opinions, there is an appreciation for Ted's platform and steadfast determination to defend the Constitution. My mother would be proud. I ask people from time to time what they think of Ted's campaign and his politics or where they think the country is going. I rarely tell people he is my cousin because I don't want that fact to change their answer. Most of the time, if someone is educated on politics they will highlight points of his campaign they like regardless of their political party affiliation. I am surprised by how many people know who he is and often they know his wife is Heidi Cruz. Heidi is Ted's secret weapon both in raising money and in foreign policy.

It will be interesting to see how this plays out. For now I will enjoy watching the show from the front row.

There's Always Hope

MY HOPE FOR THIS BOOK is to inspire you to reflect on your own life.

I don't believe in utopia, but I do believe our lives and our world would be a much better place if we took personal responsibility and accountability for our lives and our actions.

I have experienced life-changing events and I lost a few things along the way: I lost my balance, my immune system for the first year and a half, my ability to listen to warning bells for the first couple of years. Sleep. Oh, how I miss sleep. Eventually, these things have returned to me and I continue to regroup. My sleep patterns appear to be forever changed. I am a different person today than I was before I lost my parents. I am still learning what this means and how I will take life on from here.

THERE IS ALWAYS HOPE

Years ago, my close friend and the editor and champion of this book and I were commiserating about our lives. This was during my divorce and some tough personal times for her. We spent hours venting and listening to each other's stories, supporting and empathizing with each other. It was during one of these sessions that we both experienced a particularly low point. I said, "Well, there is always hope that someday life will be better, and all of this misery will be behind us." It didn't actually come out of my mouth but it is what I intended. Instead, I said "Well, there's always hope…" in a very sad, distracted kind of way. And because my friend and I both share the same dark sense of humor we both giggled. It was so pathetic, my plea for hope. Our giggles turned to laughter and before we knew it we were hysterical, crying tears of joy over the ridiculousness of it all.

This is now our favorite phrase when things get tough. It instantly brings a smile to our faces because in part it is true. Things will get better. Life will go on and you might as well laugh at the ridiculousness of it all.

In other words, don't deny your crazy; embrace it, work through it, and be better because of it.

Because there is always hope.

HELENA L. ROUHE IS A LICENSED marriage and family therapist and advanced certified EAGALA practitioner. Rouhe earned her BA in psychobiology from Pitzer College; an MA in visual processing/cognitive psychology from the University of California, Riverside; and an MA in family therapy from Chapman University.

The mind/body/spirit connection is the common thread that weaves together all of her professional and educational experiences. Rouhe excels at starting and facilitating experiential therapy programs, such as rock climbing and equine-assisted psychotherapy. Not only do these therapeutic modalities challenge personal limits, they also help to increase awareness of how a person communicates.

Rouhe lives in Coeur d'Alene, Idaho, on a small farm with her boyfriend, horses, dogs, cat, and the local wildlife who come to visit.

CPSIA information can be obtained
at www.ICGtesting.com
Printed in the USA
LVHW080159200422
716710LV00014B/788